CW00956360

# THE FIFTIES IN VOGUE

INCORPORATING
VANITY FAIR

SUMMER FASHIONS
IN AND OUT
OF TOWN

PARIS COPIES

THE BRIDE'S
BOOK

SPECIAL
FEATURES

BETTE DAVIS

LORD
DAVID CECIL

FAMOUS FACES
IN BRITISH ARTS
photographed by Penn

**Photograph on previous page by Rutledge 1951. This page Rutledge 1956.**

# THE FIFTIES IN
# VOGUE

NICHOLAS DRAKE
FOREWORD BY
AUDREY HEPBURN

HEINEMANN LONDON

William Heinemann Ltd
10 Upper Grosvenor Street, London W1X 9PA

LONDON MELBOURNE
JOHANNESBURG AUCKLAND

First published 1987

ISBN 0 434 20700 4

Designed by Steve Kibble

Printed in Hong Kong

# Contents

# FOREWORD

In 1952, when Norman Parkinson took the photograph opposite, the Belgian-born actress Audrey Hepburn had been discovered by Colette and was playing *Gigi* on Broadway: her film *Secret People* was showing in England, and she had a Paramount contract waiting. Two years later, after *Roman Holiday* and *Sabrina*, *Vogue* called her 'today's wonder-girl... She has so captured the public imagination and the mood of the time that she has established a new standard of beauty, and every other face now approximates to the "Hepburn look".' 'It is always a dramatic moment when the Phoenix rises from the ashes,' wrote Cecil Beaton. 'It took the rubble of Belgium, an English accent, and an American success to launch the striking personality that best exemplifies our new *Zeitgeist*... She is like a portrait by Modigliani where the various distortions are not only interesting in themselves but make a completely satisfying composite.'

Audrey Hepburn's every change of appearance and role was recorded in *Vogue* throughout the decade. During the filming of *Sabrina* (1954) she had enlisted a rising young Parisian couturier, Hubert de Givenchy, to design her wardrobe. It was the beginning of a lasting friendship and working relationship. Her role in the musical *Funny Face* (1957) involved modelling countless Givenchy creations – as a beatnik bookworm is transformed into the world's most glamorous mannequin by a fashion editor with 'pizzazz' and a maverick photographer, played by Fred Astaire, who were inspired by the legendary Diana Vreeland and Richard Avedon.

I remember the Fifties as a time of renewal and of regained security. Postwar austerity was fading and although the heartbreak remained, wounds were healing. There was a rebirth of opportunity, vitality and enthusiasm. The big American musicals came to London; people packed the theatres to see the twice-nightly shows of *High Button Shoes, South Pacific* and *Guys and Dolls.* Life was becoming more carefree and there was a return to laughter and gaiety.

The Fifties had a special feeling of warmth. Once again one was allowed to be optimistic about the future — the world was functioning again. Above all there was a wonderful quality of hope, born from relief and gratitude for those greatest of all luxuries — freedom and *peace.*

Audrey Hepburn

# INTRODUCTION

'After the disappointment of the post-war years it is an agreeable experience to blow one's own trumpet,' wrote Cecil Beaton in 1951. The Festival of Britain was a gesture of faith by the Labour government in a brighter, egalitarian future. Officially it was a centenary commemoration of the Great Exhibition of 1851, demonstrating British achievement in the arts, sciences and design. The organizer, Gerald Barry, promised 'fun, fantasy and colour' as 'a tonic to the nation', and all over Britain the Festival was celebrated with exhibitions and pageants, madrigals and mystery plays. In London there were pleasure gardens at Battersea Park and a large blitzed site on the South Bank of the Thames became the setting for the main exhibition. There were pavilions devoted to every aspect of the Land of Britain, from Sport to Homes and Gardens, as well as restaurants, peep shows, and a riverside promenade bright with flags and bunting. The Dome of Discovery had the largest unsupported roof in the world while the towering Skylon became the symbol of the Festival. The austere Festival Hall was the only permanent structure, and near it the Queen laid the first stone of the future National Theatre.

The design team, headed by Hugh Casson and Misha Black, gave Britons the visual stimulation they craved, with sculpture, murals, and mobiles by Moore, Hepworth, Piper, Sutherland, Topolski and Epstein. The pedestrian precinct was all grilles and screens, decks, terraces and fountains; large glasshouses seemed to float in the sky, umbrellas and parasols were suspended over tables, and visitors could rest on seats jutting out like springboards over the shimmering Thames. Walls were painted bright colours or decorated with squares of canvas pulled taut in geometric shapes; hanging Miró-like balls made a screen against the distant chimney-pots of the city. The exhibition was bright and inviting by day, but at night the effect was magical, with music and dancing under the sparkling floodlights.

***Above***, **Henry Moore's Reclining Figure, backed by an airy wall of canvas sails at the South Bank.** ***Opposite***, **'the phenomenal Skylon rides the night sky, finger-points the paradox of scientific skill made magical'. 1951. ANTHONY DENNEY.**

*Vogue* predicted the exhibition style would soon extend into home furnishing and decoration. 'If all goes well . . . what a country we shall live in, what a Britain we shall have!' wrote Marghanita Laski. 'Through all our lifetimes, the man-made objects surrounding us have been devised, not to give visual pleasure, but unconsciously to assert that we are a people wealthy, provident, puritan, insular, keeping our feet firmly on the ground and not liking to make ourselves conspicuous. Suddenly on the South Bank, we discover that, no longer wealthy, we can be imaginative and experimental and ingenious, colourful, gaudy and gay.'

The Festival turned out to be the Labour government's last fling, for in the October '51 election the Conservatives were returned to power. With the slogan 'Set the People Free' Sir Winston Churchill's new government promised a more prosperous Britain, in which the post-war restrictions associated with Labour rule would be swept aside. Identity cards and ration books were eventually abolished and a new consumer age of free enterprise, hire purchase, television and cars-for-all got under way. Affluence was the song the sirens sang in the United States, from where war and economic expansion had finally banished the Depression. Every hard-pressed country that had been brought to the point of exhaustion by the war, saw the New World as an Aladdin's cave of American goods, American entertainment, and the American style of living. Even Macmillan's famous statement that the British people had 'never had it so good' was borrowed from the chairman of the combined American labor unions.

Germany's economic miracle was financed mainly by American aid and nursed by armies of occupation. In 1951 *Vogue* peeked through the Iron Curtain in Berlin, contrasting 'the devastation, the stillness, the fear', on the Soviet side, with 'the bustling reconstruction, the bright lights, the noises of normal life' in West Berlin. 'Women are the new force in Germany!' reported *Vogue*. 'Because there are so few whole men left, women have been diverted from the one-way street called 'children, church and kitchen' to play a positive part in the future. Today they are masons, bankers, statesmen.'

***Above, left,*** **'To bring out the hidden glamour of your beauty zone', declared this Formfit bra advertisement of 1954. *Right,* Marilyn Monroe, the archetypal Fifties blonde, 'busting out all over' in *Some Like it Hot.* 1957.**
***Opposite, Vogue*** **celebrated the tenth birthday of the House of Dior with a special portrait of Christian Dior and his favourite mannequin, Renée, wearing a favourite suit from the *Libre* collection of Spring 1957. A spray of lily-of-the-valley, Dior's lucky flower, was pinned to the lapel. HENRY CLARKE.**

Joyce Cary, writing about The Revolution of the Women, observed: 'Thirty years ago college girls were told by various women's leaders that their first duty was to their sex. They had won the vote, but the women's revolution was not complete. They must now fight their way into men's careers. To have a husband, a home, and children was treachery to the cause, a piece of self-indulgence. Now we find women in all careers, and these women have homes and children. The young women not only accept the position – they choose it. Whereas thirty years ago the girl of social conscience would almost apologize for having a baby, the same girl now, more often than not, will be anxiously inquiring how many babies she can afford, and if it is possible for her to do her duty by them and her husband while keeping her job.'

Doctor Spock became the guru of childcare, adding the authority of Freudian psychology to the doctrine of putting motherhood first. None the less by the end of the decade nearly a quarter of Britain's married women were going out to work, but few of them were granted equal pay or equal opportunities. Out of 150 top jobs in the BBC, only four were held by women, and Jacqueline Wheldon, wife of BBC producer Huw Wheldon, complained about the patronizing tone in which television programmes addressed women, 'as though every woman sitting at home was a moron'. Penelope Gilliatt reported: 'A woman MP was talking undeludedly about the reverberations of Suez, and I asked her how much she had voiced her feelings in the House. "Oh," she said, shocked, "we don't speak on foreign affairs. No one would listen to a woman's views. We keep to things like food prices." Poor Mrs Pankhurst. How we have failed her.' The inimitable Anita Loos expressed her point with tongue-in-cheek, in 'The Decline and Fall of Blondes', written for *Vogue* in 1951: 'Any time we girls have to go to work the result, historically, is that we do things better than the opposite sex. I mean gentlemen will go to all the trouble of keeping office hours and holding Board Meetings and getting Mr Gallup to make a poll, and sending their Public Relations agents to Washington, in order to reach a decision which any blonde could reach, while she was refurbishing her lipstick.'

The Fifties were not a permissive era. Young couples were marrying earlier than ever and sex before marriage was frowned on by their superiors. Sex education was banned in many British schools. Despite the invention of the Pill in 1952 contraceptives were still a guilty secret and Nice Girls never went 'all the way'. But in 1953 the second Kinsey Report, *Sexual Behaviour in the Human Female*, shattered many illusions. Its evidence that women were men's sexual equals was a great leap forward for sexual frankness which also broadened the public image of the ideal woman.

Two quite different types of femininity were admired. Fifties gentlemen really did prefer blondes – three out of ten brunettes dyed their hair blonde. The careers of blonde starlets like Jayne Mansfield and Diana Dors were built on their busts' pneumatic proportions. Cantilevered and foam-rubber upholstered brassieres became best-selling beauty aids. The two universal sex symbols of the decade, Marilyn Monroe and Brigitte Bardot, brought a more intense eroticism to the screen than had ever been seen before. Their treatment of *men* as playthings was a liberation for women all over the world, who copied their looks and envied their freedom of behaviour. The phrase 'sex kitten' was coined to describe the *bébé*-faced BB, whose emancipated amorality was echoed in the bittersweet novels of the young French writer Françoise Sagan. Her stories revolved around heroines who chose and discarded their lovers at whim.

The sex kitten's antithesis was the Belgian-born actress Audrey Hepburn, whose 'appearance succeeds because it embodies the spirit of today,' wrote Cecil Beaton in *Vogue*. 'Nobody ever looked like her before World War II . . . now thousands of imitations have appeared. The woods are full of emaciated young ladies with rat-nibbled hair and moon-pale faces.' *Vogue*'s model queens were also accorded film star status. Barbara Goalen and Fiona Campbell-Walter were legendary beauties who personified the air of aloof sophistication that spelt elegance throughout the decade. Seldom photographed without long gloves and a parure of jewels they made the simplest off-the-peg dress look like a couture model and were equally convincing in a mackintosh or a tiara. Other star models and actresses, like Suzy Parker and Ann Gunning, Grace Kelly and Claire Bloom, shared this look of cool composure and high caste: they were symbols, not of sex, but of high style.

Fashion in the Fifties had never been more feminine – the success of Christian Dior's extravagantly romantic New Look of

1947, with its waspie waists and billowing full skirts, reasserted the dominance of Paris fashion and established Dior as its dictator until his death in 1957. The rapidly expanding ready-to-wear market in Britain and America depended upon Paris innovations – looks and lines followed one another in quick succession, grabbing newspaper headlines and making last year's wardrobe obsolete. Unless you dressed at Chanel, who in 1954 re-introduced the comfortable cardigan suits she had invented in the Twenties, Paris clothes were conspicuously impractical for working women. Boned and strapless 'self-supporting' bodices made it difficult to bend and corsets pinched the waist. 'Where has the waist gone?' asked *Vogue* in 1951, and answered 'Anywhere but where you expect it.' There were heavy pyramid coats with jutting collars and pencil-slim hobble skirts, or flared skirts that stood out like tents, supported by layers of underskirts in the new 'crackle' nylon. Beneath seamless stockings of sheer nylon were shoes with stiletto heels which ruined floors in the name of style.

The development of washable drip-dry fibres like Terylene and Courtelle, together with new systems of mass production, made the average Englishwoman among the best-dressed in the world and transformed the working girl's wardrobe, making it possible for her to wear a different outfit every day. For the first time the young had a fashion identity of their own. The word 'teenager' itself was an import from America – before the war there had been only 'girls' and 'youths'. Their independence was based on their earning capacity; by 1959 £8 a week for a boy, £6 for a girl. A popular song was 'You gotta have something in the bank, Frank' and now there were jobs, shorter working hours, and somewhere to go afterwards. Jazz clubs, where students jived with a girl in one hand and a bottle in the other, dance halls with a skiffle group or a rock'n'roll band, clubs where juke boxes were fed by motor-cycle boys in studded leather jackets, jackboots and blue jeans, and all day long there were coffee bars, where bearded 'beats' sat in corners complaining about life. Soon the West End was a neon world of gleaming glass and chrome Espressos, Wimpys, Bar-B-Ques, Moo-Cow Milk Bars and Chicken Inns.

'When people of an older generation see a boy in sharp clothes, with his hand in his pocket, they are apt to suppose he is reaching for his flick-knife,' cautioned *Vogue*, 'in fact he is more likely to be digging out the price of a record or a coke.' Among the teenagers it was the men's appearance rather than the girls' that identified their group, whether the draped jackets, greased quiffs, and suede shoes of the Teddy Boys or the sloppy sweaters, beards and sandals of the 'weekend beats'. It was a reversal of *Vogue*'s world in which women wore the conspicuous fashions and men were the decorous background.

These teenage fashions were the first to begin in the street and work upward into *Vogue*, and by 1959 the magazine was asking questions about the new trends. 'What does fashion represent? Decoration? Armour? Disguise? A mood of society? For millions of working teenagers now clothes like these are the biggest pastime in life: a symbol of independence, and the fraternity mark of an age-group . . . The origins of the teenage look are urban and working-class . . . but it has been taken up with alacrity by the King's Road. Contrariwise, it is itself influenced by the romantic concept of Chelsea. It owes nothing to Paris or Savile Row; something to entertainment idols (the Tommy Steele haircut . . . the Bardot sex babe look); much to Italy, and surprisingly little to America.'

***Opposite***, **'Summer means, for millions of Americans, varying proportions of baseball, hot dogs, and Coca-Cola,' wrote *Vogue* in 1952. PENN.**
***Above***, **the teenage sharp cat's quiffed hair-cut and 'sumptuous pointed shoes'. The three-wheeled Italian Isetta, 'a revolutionary new car'. 1954.**

A new generation of art school trained designers gave the young fashion movement its greatest impetus, turning out uninhibited designs for non-establishment fashion. In 1953 *Vogue* started a regular Young Idea feature and in 1955 Mary Quant opened Bazaar in the King's Road, selling the naïvely simple clothes that would eventually make her the major fashion force in the world outside Paris. Her shop became the social centre for the bohemian Chelsea Set – the new version of the Bright Young Things. They liked to navigate Vespa motor scooters or bubble cars around the King's Road where small 'peasanty' restaurants with handwritten menus and bright little boutiques with help-yourself clothes rails blossomed among the grocers' shops and artists' pubs. The Chelsea Set,

whose affairs dominated the gossip columns, formed a new café society who liked to rub shoulders with the working-class playwrights of the English Stage Company at the Royal Court Theatre in Sloane Square.

The ultimate bohemians were the American 'Beats' – a generation of college drop-outs who lived nomadic and amoral lives across the States. They discovered marijuana, published poetry and read the Beats' Bible, Jack Kerouac's *On the Road*. The Existentialists of Left Bank Paris and the Hippies of the Sixties were their nearest predecessors and successors. Adopting the argot of modern black jazzmen, whose music made them 'flip', they addressed each other as 'man' and referred to themselves as 'cats' who 'dug groovy chicks' and were bugged by 'squares' and the need to earn 'bread'. The nightclub monologuist Mort Sahl and Tom Lehrer, a Harvard maths graduate turned songwriter, were 'subversive' satirists who became heroes of the Beat generation.

In Britain a new group of writers, disillusioned with British politics and cant, attacked the old order of privilege and genteel complacency. In 1954 Kingsley Amis' anti-hero *Lucky Jim* made his debut. John Osborne's *Look Back in Anger* was presented at the Royal Court in 1956 and soon after Colin Wilson, the working-class philosopher-author of *The Outsider* achieved overnight celebrity as a real-life example of an Angry Young Man. 'The English Stage Company has revived the contemporary theatre single-handed,' reported *Vogue* in 1958. 'Notably it has avoided the usual impasse of avant-garde theatre, where the minority is so *avant* and the majority so guarded that useful communication between them never begins.' The Royal Court's influence seeped steadily across London to the West End, and theatre managers, at first apprehensive about losing their lovely drawing-rooms, began installing kitchen sinks with conviction. *Vogue*'s readers were offered reduced price tickets at the Royal Court and Antony Armstrong-Jones immortalized George Devine and his entire company aboard a Sloane Square bus. The following year he photographed Bernard Miles with a boatful of colleagues on the Thames at Puddle Dock, beside his new Mermaid Theatre. Designed on Elizabethan principles with an open stage, inside the walls of an old warehouse, it was the first new theatre to be built in London for thirty years and was financed entirely by public subscription.

Radio drama could be as avant-garde as the theatre. The BBC commissioned and broadcast plays by Samuel Beckett, Harold Pinter, and, most celebrated of all, Dylan Thomas. *Under Milk Wood* was first performed the year after his death in 1953, narrated by Richard Burton. Radio broadcast the first situation comedies, later to become the staple fodder of television. Tony Hancock's gagless characterization in 'Hancock's Half-Hour' and the anarchic wit of 'The Goon Show' contributed to a golden age of radio comedy. Television was initially considered a minor offshoot of the serious medium of radio. The blandness of the BBC's programmes kept its social status low and intellectual opinion tended to ignore it, or to look in just for cricket and coronations. It was after the Coronation, which received full coverage by the BBC, that the immense public which for the first time had watched television presentation at its best began flocking to buy or rent television sets.

The advent of commercial television in 1955 – a national disaster, according to the Labour Party – attracted millions more viewers, and within four years had poached 70 per cent of the BBC's audience. 'The stars of television are called (revealingly) "personalities",' wrote Isabel Quigly in *Vogue*. 'They don't have to know much, to do much, or to act much. They simply have to *be*.' Gilbert Harding became Britain's most popular television

***Above*, Joan Littlewood, directing her Theatre Workshop company: 'a small, dauntless band of idealists, clinging to the belief that theatre is a popular art'. 1959. EUAN DUFF. *Below*, a 'family portrait' of writers, actors, and directors from the Royal Court, including Joan Plowright, John Osborne, Tony Richardson, George Devine, and John Arden. 1958. TONY ARMSTRONG-JONES.**

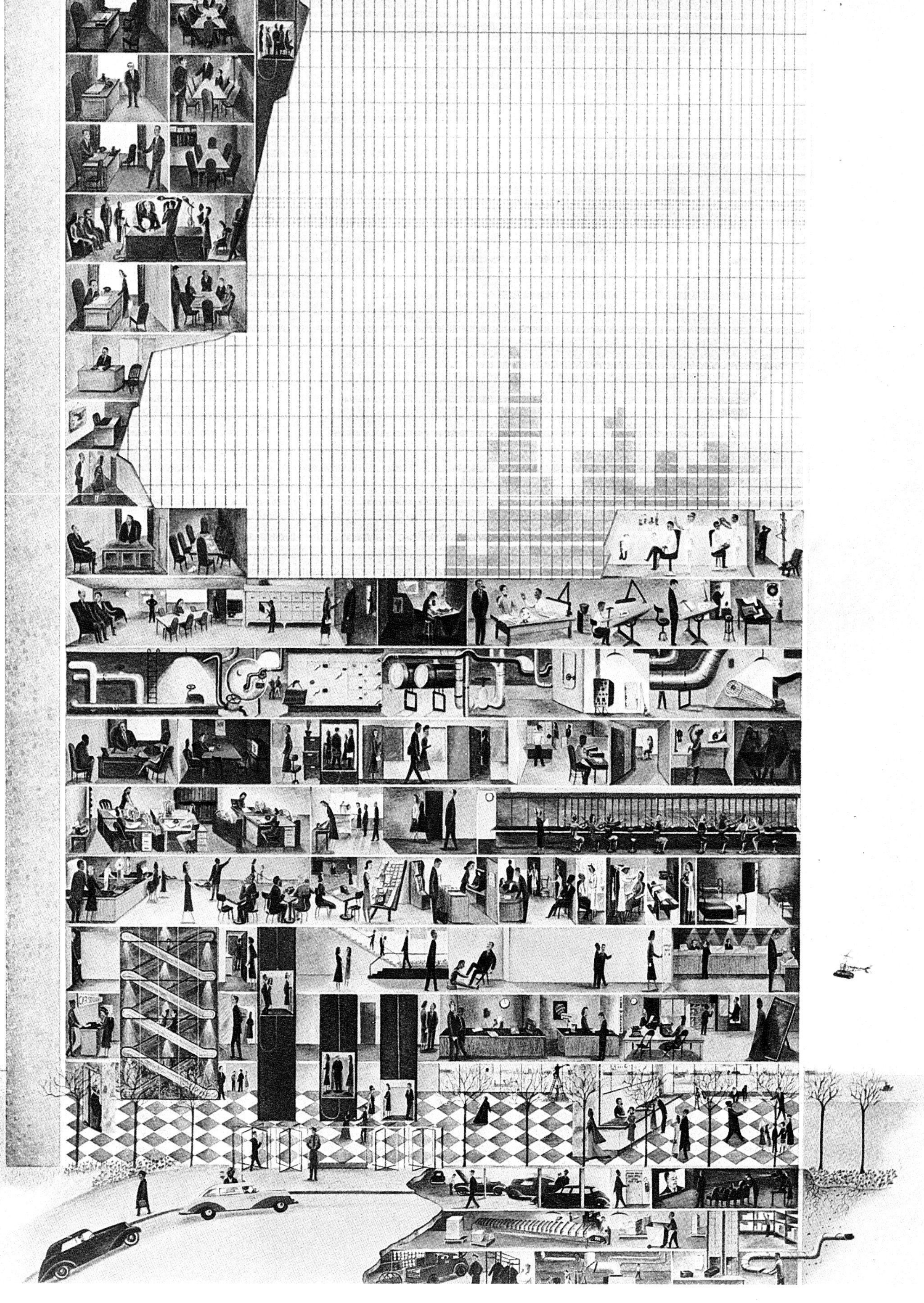

*Above*, a cross section of the interior of the two-year-old United Nations Secretariat building in New York: 'this cool, handsome slab of a building (shaped like an ant-palace) gives no sense of the brimming hubbub actually within its walls'. 1952. MARGARET BLOY GRAHAM.

*Above*, the American automobile industry had become as style-conscious as the fashion business: 'a blend of caramel colours seated on the wing-back formation of the 1959 Chevrolet Impala convertible. New beauty point of this car: a tray in the dash that could be a dressing table.' 1959. RAWLINGS.

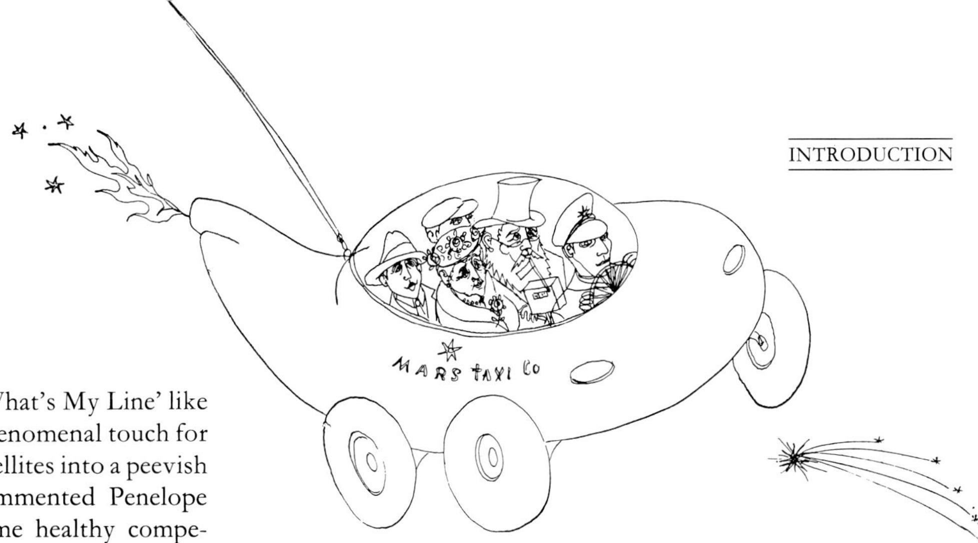


*Above*, **'Our party boarded a pressurized car . . .' One of the whimsical sketches illustrating Kenneth Heuer's projected 'Vacation on Mars'. 1953. J.J. WATTS.**

'personality', presiding over the panel game 'What's My Line' like a latterday Dr Johnson. 'Only an age with a phenomenal touch for dullness could have turned the first artificial satellites into a peevish panel of cosmic television personalities,' commented Penelope Gilliatt. Independent television provided some healthy competition for the BBC and helped to raise the standards of drama and current affairs programmes with Independent's 'Armchair Theatre' and the BBC's 'Panorama'. By 1959 26 million Britons were tuning in every evening to a reliable diet of high-pressure advertising and American or home-grown versions of gangster series, hospital dramas, situation comedies, Westerns and, most popular of all, give-away quiz shows. Aldous Huxley's prophetic 'Age of Television' had become a reality.

An eclectic selection of writers contributed to *Vogue*'s feature pages, which were edited by Siriol Hugh-Jones and later by Penelope Gilliatt, who was to marry John Osborne. Brendan Behan, Jonathan Miller, Dylan Thomas, Laurie Lee and Lord David Cecil all wrote for *Vogue*. Kingsley Amis decried 'The New Puritans'; Christopher Logue compiled a 'Plain Girl's Guide to Poetry'; Malcolm Muggeridge defined 'The Art of Noncomforming'; and Iris Murdoch explained 'What I See in Cinema'. In 1951 *Vogue* initiated an annual talent contest, which offered would-be journalists the chance of a job on the magazine. Early winners included Anne Scott-James, Isabel Quigly, and Edward Lucie-Smith. The winner of American *Vogue*'s 1951 Prix de Paris was a young college graduate, Jacqueline Bouvier.

'It took the brief, frustrating period of petrol rationing to bring home to us that a car really does add another dimension to our lives', wrote *Vogue* in 1957, and cars were now part of more women's lives than ever before. *Vogue*'s regular motoring feature invited personalities like Lady Barnett to define 'What I want from my car' and assess the latest models. The American automobile industry became as style conscious as the fashion business, with designs changing every other year. Motels sprang up across the United States to accommodate the many long-distance travellers. European motoring holidays were as popular as ever – *Vogue* proposed numerous routes through 'Europe by car and sight-seeing trips designed by 'inventive motorists' like Christian Dior. Parking meters and multi-storey garages were introduced to help decongest the cities which motorways were beginning to connect. In 1959 the decade's most original innovation in transport, the air-cushioned Hovercraft, made its first Channel crossing. Destined, of course, to carry cars.

Science and technology leapt forward in the Fifties, revolutionizing human mobility and communications. Atomic power stations promised cheap and plentiful energy and nuclear-powered ships and submarines were launched – *Vogue* nominated America's Seawolf submarine (1959) 'a masterpiece of planning'. After the excitement of Hillary and Tenzing's conquest of Everest in 1953 people's attention turned to the glamour of space exploration. In 1957 the first Soviet Sputniks orbited the earth and, stung by their own failure to launch satellites, the United States began frantically training astronauts to beat the Russians into space and to the moon – the space race was on. The fascination with space created a worldwide boom in UFO-spotting; hardly a week passed without press reports of someone claiming to have seen a flying saucer. UFO societies were established and books on the extraterrestrial flooded the market. There were both sceptics and believers about the phenomenon's existence but *Vogue* remained neutral, publishing a satirical essay which referred to Willow-pattern saucers and cups, and also proposing a scientifically researched 'Vacation on Mars' by a Fellow of the Royal Astronomical Society.

The Eurovision television network was established in 1954 and direct transatlantic telephone service began in 1956. But the most dynamic contribution to world communications was the advent of jet passenger travel, pioneered by the De Havilland Comet, which began the first scheduled jet service between London and Johannesburg in 1952. Transatlantic jet service was inaugurated in 1958, the first year in which more people crossed the Atlantic by plane than by ship. The jet had now taken over from the luxury liner as the smartest way to travel; the airlines competed in pampering their passengers – PanAm boasted catering by Maxim's of Paris – and teenage girls dreamt of becoming air hostesses.

*Vogue*'s intrepid contributors travelled the world: Truman Capote enticed readers to Tangier, 'to be swallowed in the mists of the Casbah'; John Gielgud donned carnival costume for the Mardi Gras in Haiti; V.S. Naipaul cruised the Caribbean and learnt the art of calypso on an island in the sun; and Peter Ustinov devised an idiosyncratic 'Young smuggler's guide to the Customs'. Tour operators introduced pre-paid package holidays and with time and cost reduced even the most ambitious destinations became accessible. 'The aeroplane and modern shipping line have made it possible to pack into a few weeks what would once have been years of voyaging,' enthused *Vogue* in 1957, suggesting a 23,000 mile, eight-stop 'whirl around the Pacific' – Australia, Japan, Hong Kong and Fiji were now just across the international date line. 'Nothing any longer seems impossible. Next year, the Pacific; the year after that, the moon.'

# THE CORONATION

On January 31, 1952 the King appeared on the roof of London Airport to wave goodbye to Princess Elizabeth and Prince Philip, who were off on a Commonwealth tour. One week later the nation was deeply shocked by his sudden death at Sandringham and Britain's new young Queen began her flight home from Africa. George VI left behind him an immensely popular monarchy. *Vogue* mourned the death of the dearly loved king who had 'maintained the traditions of the First Gentleman of the land and wedded them to those of the first public servant'. A.L. Rowse welcomed 'the young woman so well-known and loved all over the English speaking world [who] succeeds to the dazzling and lonely position, with all its cares and responsibilities, that has been awaiting her since childhood.' Like her father, the Queen was determined to keep abreast of progress and to set an example of service and personal dedication to her subjects all over the world. Symbolically the new reign, hailed by some as the new Elizabethan Age, was heralded by Edmund Hillary's conquest of Everest.

*Vogue* joined in the 'Coronation fever' that gripped the nation, reporting on balloting in the House of Lords for Coronation seats in Westminster Abbey, the chances of five-year-old Prince Charles attending the ceremony and the numerous rather sad advertisements in *The Times* to buy or sell tiaras, ceremonial swords and 'Countess's Coronation robe, medium size, only worn once'.

The BBC's faultess presentation of the Coronation gave a television audience of over twenty million Britons a better view than the privileged participants, who were observed in the Abbey by Cecil Beaton. 'This is history, but it is of today, living and new. There is no pretence or make-believe about this great display. Each incident in this long ritual is in itself a symbol of what is noblest in us. These people have been born to perform these offices – to present a glove, an orb or a sword to the Queen. They have been rehearsing their roles since birth,' he wrote in *Vogue*. 'This wonderful ceremony takes the mind back through a thousand years, yet it is as fresh and inspiring as some great histrionic ritual, enacted upon a spontaneous impulse of genius.' Elizabeth Bowen joined the great crowd of spectators in the Mall as they awaited the Queen's golden coach:

***Opposite,*** **Her Majesty Queen Elizabeth II, an historic Coronation day portrait, photographed at Buckingham Palace by Cecil Beaton, who admired the Queen's 'Byzantine magnificence' wearing rich brocade and the Imperial Crown.** ***Above, Vogue's*** **June Coronation issue cover, an ornate celebration in cut glass, photographed by Norman Parkinson, who also commemorated some of the dignitaries in the Abbey.**

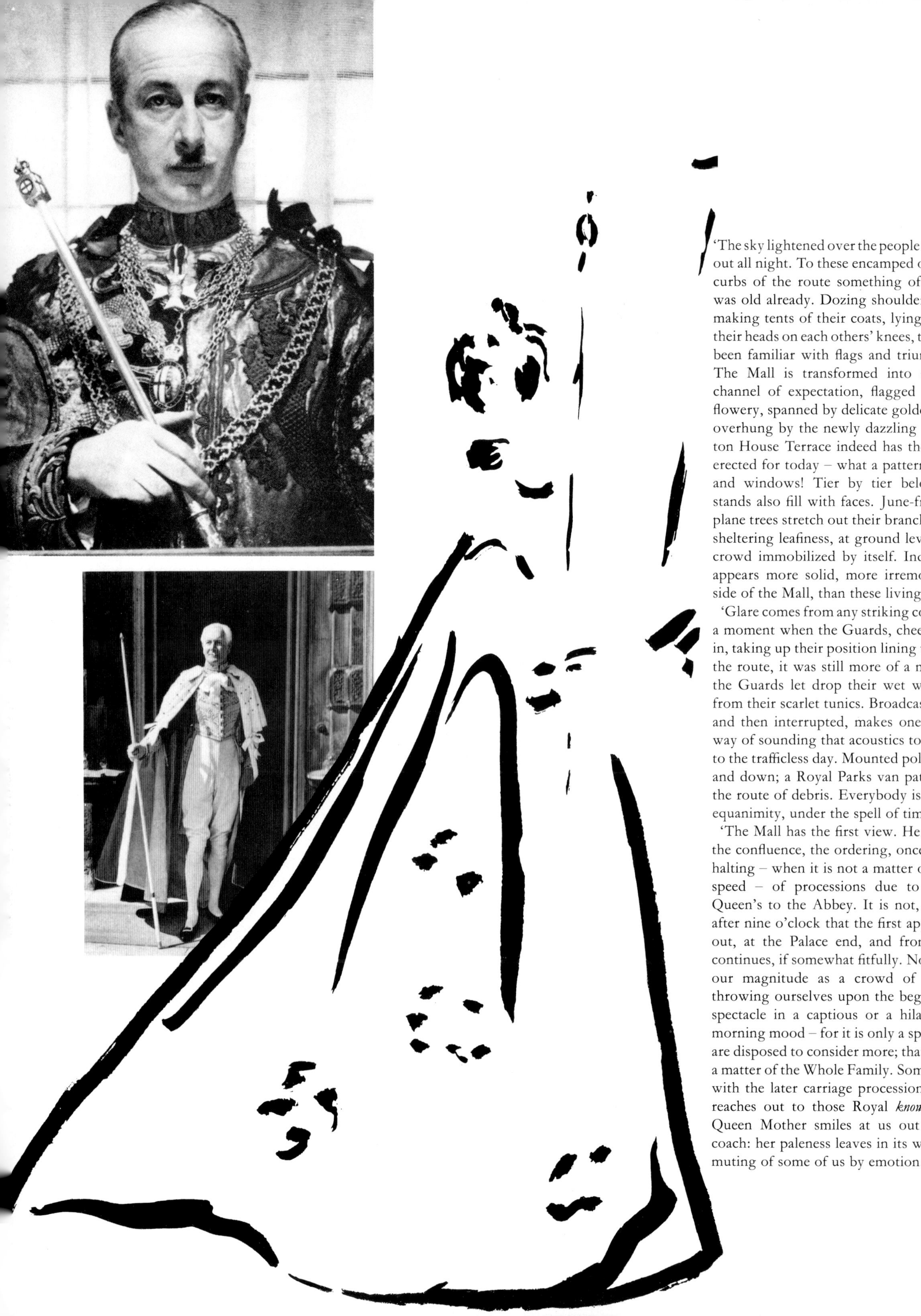

'The sky lightened over the people who had been out all night. To these encamped ones along the curbs of the route something of the morning was old already. Dozing shoulder to shoulder, making tents of their coats, lying waiting with their heads on each others' knees, they have long been familiar with flags and triumphal arches. The Mall is transformed into an enormous channel of expectation, flagged and peopled, flowery, spanned by delicate golden hoops, and overhung by the newly dazzling façades. Carlton House Terrace indeed has the air of being erected for today – what a pattern of balconies and windows! Tier by tier below them the stands also fill with faces. June-fresh, ranks of plane trees stretch out their branches; under the sheltering leafiness, at ground level, packs in a crowd immobilized by itself. Indeed, nothing appears more solid, more irremovable, either side of the Mall, than these living walls.

'Glare comes from any striking colour; if it was a moment when the Guards, cheered, marched in, taking up their position lining this section of the route, it was still more of a moment when the Guards let drop their wet weather cloaks from their scarlet tunics. Broadcast music, now and then interrupted, makes one aware by its way of sounding that acoustics too are peculiar to the trafficless day. Mounted police jogtrot up and down; a Royal Parks van patrols, clearing the route of debris. Everybody is waiting with equanimity, under the spell of timelessness.

'The Mall has the first view. Here takes place the confluence, the ordering, once or twice the halting – when it is not a matter of car-smooth speed – of processions due to precede the Queen's to the Abbey. It is not, indeed, long after nine o'clock that the first applause breaks out, at the Palace end, and from then on it continues, if somewhat fitfully. Now do we feel our magnitude as a crowd of thousands – throwing ourselves upon the beginning of the spectacle in a captious or a hilarious unpent morning mood – for it is only a spectacle till we are disposed to consider more; that is, when it is a matter of the Whole Family. Something enters with the later carriage processions; each of us reaches out to those Royal *known* faces. The Queen Mother smiles at us out of the glass coach: her paleness leaves in its wake a hush, a muting of some of us by emotion.

*Opposite,* photographs and drawing by Cecil Beaton: *Top left,* The Garter Principal King of Arms, the Hon. Sir George Bellew, CVO, who was largely responsible for planning and organizing the intricate ceremonial of the Coronation. *Centre left,* The Lord Great Chamberlain, the Marquess of Cholmondeley, who was in close attendance upon the Queen during the ceremony. *Right,* the Queen carrying the Sceptre with Cross and the Rod with Dove. *Left,* the Archbishop of Canterbury, the Most Rev. and Right Hon. Dr Geoffrey Francis Fisher, who was solely responsible for church liturgy at the Coronation. *Above,* Bearer of the Union Standard, Captain John Dymoke, the Queen's Champion. NORMAN PARKINSON.

***Above,*** **a group of pages drawn by Cecil Beaton.** ***Right,*** **The Lord High Chancellor, the Right Hon. Lord Simonds of Sparsholt, with his Purse, symbol of his position as Keeper of the Great Seal of England.** ***Below,*** **Marshall of the Royal Air Force, the Viscount Portal of Hungerford, bearer of the Sceptre with the Cross.** ***Opposite,*** **the Maids of Honour, Queen Elizabeth's Train Bearers.** ***From left to right.*** **Lady Anne Coke, Lady Jane Heathcote-Drummond-Willoughby, Lady Rosemary Spencer-Churchill, Lady Moyra Hamilton, and Lady Jane Vane-Tempest-Stewart. CECIL BEATON.**

After a pause, Her Majesty's procession ... There is an incredibility, now that it is in view, about the advancing stage coach, the eight grey horses, the four golden tritons. Hearts, as though not ready yet for the moment, stand still. This is pure fairy tale. That impression of radiance left by the young beauty seated beside her husband makes us want back the moment to live again.

The coach takes its golden, surrounded way down the perspective, vanishes with a final gleam under the Admiralty Arch. Have we, till now, envisaged her destination, or, still more, the isolation, in any human sense, of the journey she is about to make? What has to be the extent of her dedication, only she knows. How dare we compute the weight of the Crown? Though by love surrounded, she is not to be accompanied on her whole way. We thousands left behind in the Mall are now let known that the Queen has entered the Abbey – here, now, in the open air, under the changing sky, we must consider the sacrament of the Coronation. Broadcast, the words of the service sound here between the double lines of the Mall plane trees – and yet, no, listen; the beautifully spoken words carry ancient reverberations of the Abbey. As the Queen is being anointed, the sun comes out and for a minute floods over everything; before we know, rain has begun to fall, sighing soft at first, glistening on the umbrellas crowdedly unfurled on the speechless stands; then thickening, muffling the forty-one gun salutes at the Queen's crowning. This rain, earlier so much dreaded, seems to enhance a sort of reconciled calm; we have it in common with one another.

Look, the rain has stopped; the late afternoon Mall – wet flags and crowds, glistening trees and arches – stands out in dauntingly splendid and candid light. Her Majesty's two-and-a-half-mile long procession begins to enter, at the Admiralty end of the cleared length. There is the pulse of the endless marching, rank on rank, race on race, uncased colours, medals, men mounted, unswerving horses, bearskins, turbans, bayonets, bands. Eight home-going grey horses; four gold tritons. Seen through alternate windows of the coach is the head bowing the steadily balanced crown. All the long taut straight way to the Palace gates in a continuous moment of Recognition: we behold ELIZABETH, our undoubted Queen.'

# FACES IN VOGUE

Princess Margaret was the leading social figure of the era; on her twenty-first birthday in 1951 *Vogue* described her as 'a fairy tale princess by right of birth and beauty who has come to stand arbiter of taste in fashion and behaviour among her contemporaries, and thus become the focus of all young admiring eyes.' Her romance with the dashing but divorced Group-Captain Peter Townsend, a former royal equerry, eventually ended in a formal statement of renunciation in 1955. At the end of the decade the Princess proved her unconventionality by marrying the photographer Antony Armstrong-Jones.

There was a new social fluidity in this era of newly acquired affluence. Property developers and oil magnates like Charles Clore and Paul Getty, tagged The Richest Man in the World, purchased country estates and entertained royalty at their much publicized parties. The Greek shipping tycoon Aristotle Onassis entertained Sir Winston Churchill on his yacht and kept the gossip columns agog over his stormy romance with *diva* Maria Callas. The flamboyant Lady Docker became 'a fable of our age', flaunting such excesses as her gold-plated Daimler upholstered in zebra skin. Danger-loving playboys like Prince Aly Khan and Porfirio Rubirosa enlivened international society with their amorous exploits until both were tragically killed in car crashes. The Duke and Duchess of Windsor each published their versions of the marriage-of-the-century story. Wallis remained an avid party-goer and feuded with social arbitress Elsa Maxwell.

'One day in March the great gates of Buckingham Palace swing open. The procession of limousines forms up the Mall, and the first of the year's débutantes make their breathless curtsies to the Queen, then spill prettily as a carnival of flowers on to the smooth green lawns to take tea and chocolate cake. And so, with gentleness and great dignity, another season begins,' wrote *Vogue* in 1956. Two years later the tradition of the débutantes' court presentation that had begun in 1786 came to an end. But the London Season survived the loss of the symbolic curtsy to the throne and glamorous debs continued to be news, in gossip columns and in *Vogue*.

Two of the most popular from the last court presentation seasons were Frances Sweeney, daughter of Margaret, Duchess of Argyll, who married the Duke of Rutland, and Henrietta

Tiarks, who became the very last Deb of the Year and later married the Marquis of Tavistock. A less conventional débutante was Suna Portman, heiress to the Portman estates, who became a beatnik fashion leader of the bohemian Chelsea Set. Some débutantes became popular symbols of romance by running away for love, though usually with Old Etonians. Seventeen-year-old Bolivian heiress Isobel Patino eloped to Gretna Green with Jimmy Goldsmith, and Tessa Kennedy ran away to the West Indies with Dominic Elwes. Fifteen-year-old Ira von Furstenberg scandalized society when she received Papal dispensation to marry Prince von Hohenlohe in 1955. International beauties were the Grace Kelly-like Dolores Guinness, who married her stepbrother, and the swan-necked Donna Marella Caracciolo, who married Fiat heir Gianni Agnelli in 1954. In the best Twenties chorus girl tradition, models like Bronwen Pugh and the classically beautiful Fiona Campbell-Walter married aristocrats – Lord Astor and the Croesus-rich Baron Thyssen.

***Opposite,* 'H.R.H. Princess Margaret, whose portrait by the Duchess of Kent we now publish, celebrated her twenty-second birthday on August 21'. 1952.**
***Right,* 'The Duchess of Kent, whose father held several exhibitions of his paintings, loves to exercise her skill as a portrait painter, using her family and friends as models'. 1953. CECIL BEATON. *Above,* the Duchess of Windsor, sketched by René Bouché, holding a lorgnette designed for her by Cartier. 1955.**

*Above,* Mrs William 'Babe' Paley, whose husband founded Columbia Broadcasting System. She was one of the three beautiful Cushing sisters from Boston and a former *Vogue* fashion editor. 1954. PENN. *Opposite,* Mrs Winston 'C. Z.' Guest, 'one of the great American fashion personalities, whose trademark is her beautifully understated chic', looking as ethereal as a wood-sprite in an imaginative summer headdress created by Cecil Beaton. 1959. CECIL BEATON.

*Vogue*'s star models of the Fifties were legendary beauties who personified the air of aloof sophistication that spelt elegance throughout the decade: *Opposite*, Barbara Goalen, photographed by Norman Parkinson in 1956. *Above*, Fiona Campbell-Walter, 'as finely bred as a champion greyhound', photographed in 1954 by Cecil Beaton.

*Opposite*, Henrietta Tiarks made her debut in 1957 and became the very last Deb of the Year. She is now the Marchioness of Tavistock. 1958. RUTLEDGE. *Above*, Vicomtesse Jacqueline de Ribes, photographed by Antony Armstrong-Jones in 1959. 'A great beauty, her high cheekbones and slanted dark green eyes give her a mysterious, exotic look'. For three decades one of the world's best-dressed women, she has recently become a couturier in her own right.

*Opposite,* Donna Marella Agnelli, looking like a latter-day Boldini, photographed by Henry Clarke in 1956. *Above,* Mme Arturo Lopez-Willshaw, the elegant Chilean-born wife of the great South American collector; they turned their house at Neuilly into a miniature Versailles. 1956. HENRY CLARKE.

*Opposite,* Mrs Leopold Stokowski, formerly Gloria Vanderbilt, 'has highly individual looks, an exotic beauty. The wife of the famous conductor counters his music with painting and is the mother of two small sons'. 1953. CECIL BEATON. *Above,* Countess Mona Bismark, formerly Mrs Harrison Williams, known for her chic and beauty since the Thirties: 'the extraordinary aquamarine eyes still dominate a face of almost flawless perfection'. Photographed by Cecil Beaton at her villa in Capri. 1959.

*Above*, Mrs John F. Kennedy and Mrs Michael T. Canfield, formerly the Misses Jacqueline and Lee Bouvier of Washington D.C. 'They're the wives, respectively, of the young senator from Massachusetts and of Harper Brothers' young London representative.' 1955. HORST. *Opposite*, Mrs Stavros Niarchos and Mrs Aristotle Onassis: 'The two lovely Livanos sisters are both statuesque on the Tanagra-figurine scale: small-scaled delicacy.' 1957. HENRY CLARKE.

*Above*, 'Two of the world's ranking beauties – Mexican-born Mrs Loel, Gloria Guinness (seated), who dresses with quietly declared elegance, and her daughter, Mrs Patrick Guinness, the former Countess Dolores von Furstenberg. They are photographed in Paris in dresses designed by Balenciaga.' 1957. HENRY CLARKE. *Opposite*, Clarissa Churchill, niece of the Prime Minister Sir Winston Churchill and at one time *Vogue*'s feature editor. She later became Mrs Anthony Eden. 1950. CECIL BEATON.

*Above*, Mrs David Bruce, the wife of the American Ambassador to France, photographed by Cecil Beaton at the Ambassador's official residence in Paris. 1950. *Opposite*, the Wyndham-Quin sisters: (left to right) Mrs John Wyndham, Lady Cranborne and Lady Roderic Pratt photographed in a setting and in poses deliberately reminiscent of the famous portrait of their second cousins, *The Wyndham Sisters*, by John Singer Sargent. 1950. CECIL BEATON.

# SOCIETY ABROAD

*Above*, Sir Alexander Korda's yacht at Venice and aboard it, *far right, from left to right*, Graham Greene, William Paley and Sir Alexander Korda. 1953. LELAND HAYWARD. *Right*, the Duchesse de Brissac (the Duc is in the background), 'one of the best-dressed women' on the Aegean cruise organized by Elsa Maxwell, *opposite below left* (with Princess Maria Pia of Yugoslavia), for Mr and Mrs Stavros Niarchos, *opposite right*, in costume for their Corfu party. 1955. HENRY CLARKE. *Opposite above*, Mr and Mrs Stavros Niarchos sketched by René Bouché on their luxurious three-masted schooner, the *Creole*. 1958.

'One of the chief pleasures of travel is to savour the difference between "at home" and "abroad",' observed *Vogue* in 1955, and with the advent of jet travel in the Fifties society became truly international. The Jet Set world was an endless playground of glamorous resorts stretching from Newport and Nassau to Monte Carlo and Montego Bay.

In 1955 the ubiquitous Elsa Maxwell helped Stavros Niarchos to 'interest travellers in Greek tourism' by inviting a boatland of over one hundred celebrity socialites to cruise the Aegean – 'where all the shores are pearl, the water nectar and the rocks pure gold'. The Duchess of Windsor was not invited and is said to have called the group 'Elsa's Zoo'. Sir Alexander Korda was more selective when he entertained the Leland Haywards, the William Paleys and Graham Greene to a four-week jaunt up the Adriatic on his rebuilt anti-submarine boat.

Jamaica was the favourite haunt of those seeking winter sun. Noel Coward spent a good part of the year there, enjoying 'the lovely cosiness of the rich living quite simply' with friends like Lord Beaverbrook and Lady Rothermere. She married Ian Fleming on the island in 1952 and Fleming later described some typical Jamaican days in the Caribbean's international habitués for *Vogue*:

'Noel Coward gets up at six and works until twelve every day. Lord Beaverbrook holds suave but impish sway over Montego with that hectoring cajolery which has made him great in a larger pond even than the Caribbean. Some famous English actors and actresses, including Beatrice Lillie, Gladys Cooper and Adrienne Allen are also making it their headquarters.

'Prince and Princess Liechtenstein ride over their fine properties in the morning and in the evening play gentle but energetic tennis with the notables of Port Maria. Edward Molyneux paints beautifully and plans his new house at "Mo Bay". Oliver Messel just paints beautifully. The Vincent Astors admire their superb view and spend a lot of time (I assume) motoring down to it to bathe. Millicent Rogers and her son Peter Salm embellish the golden sands, and Mr Otis Q. Phelps, with Mrs Phelps, tours the island indefatigably in a 1930 Lincoln taxi.

'Still others like myself spend most of the day, way down the coast, spear-fishing on the reef and telling visitors, as did Cecil Beaton when he

came to stay, that sticks and stones may hurt one's bones but not the grimaces on barracuda faces. In one room Rosamund Lehmann is working at her new novel and in another Loelia Westminster is exercising one of the talents from her quiver, on a landscape with figures.'

For those who preferred some winter snow, St Moritz remained a legend among resorts, familiar faces returning each year to the old-fashioned Palace Hotel. From late morning to eight at night men and women from all Europe, North and South America lived in ski clothes whether they skied or not. The women dressed with unbeatable chic in cashmere sweaters, heavy Italian silk shirts and tailored ski trousers. For dinner, they changed into separates to eat in town, or full-blown evening dress to eat at the Palace Hotel. After breakfast, the day proceeded gently up the mountain to the exclusive Corviglia Club, where one could enjoy a buffet luncheon served on a terrace in the sun. Later hot-chocolate hour crowded Hanselmann's famous pastry shop, and then it was cocktails at the Palace bar until time to change for dinner. The Chesa Veglia night club, set in an old Swiss chalet, provided food and Swiss music.

**Jamaican habitués: *left*, Cecil Beaton photographed by Lady Rothermere. Beaton photographed his friends Beatrice Lillie, *top*, with a Jamaican friend, and, *above*, Ian Fleming. *Opposite*, Noel Coward, at the piano, with Mrs John C. Wilson (formerly Princess Natasha Paley) and Graham Payn. 1951.**

'For almost a century the French Riviera, the first resort of the internationals, has meant pervasive gaiety, lemon trees, salty air, sun even in winter – against a spectacular backcloth of mountains and the Mediterranean,' declared *Vogue* in 1958. Here had come painters and writers, Russian grand dukes, deposed kings, beauties, the rich from every continent. To them all, Riviera life – the Provençal villages, the villas, the yachts, the small motor boats clacking across the harbour – combined the enchantment of nature and worldly pleasures.

Most famous of the villa owners was Somerset Maugham, who settled down in 1926 at his tall, white Villa Mauresque at St Jean Cap Ferrat, living there with his collection of paintings, including a Picasso, a Renoir and a Gauguin which he bought in Tahiti. Not far from him lived Lady Kenmare and her son Roderick Cameron, who after the war had made a Palladian villa out of a bombed house with an extraordinary vista, La Fiorentina. Prince Rainier and Princess Grace built an isolated stone house on Mont Agel, and came down sometimes to cruise in their sailing schooner.

'With a smack like a big theatrical opening' the

**Familiar St Moritz faces photographed by Henry Clarke. *Above,* Countess Brando Brandolini, 'one of the best-dressed women in St Moritz'. *Top left,* Mrs Philip Isles. *Top right,* Mrs Stavros Niarchos and Mrs A. Onassis. *Centre right,* Mr and Mrs André Embiricos. *Below right,* Mme Jacques Fath. 1952. *Opposite,* Riviera personalities: Their Serene Highnesses, Prince Rainier and Princess Grace of Monaco, sketched by René Bouché in the drawing room of their Palace. 1958.**

season at Monte Carlo opened in July with a gala at the summer gambling Casino. From the beach road, the Casino looked like an old factory, but inside was a glory of glamour, massed flowers, uniformed servants, and a suntanned crowd of film stars, movie producers, bankers, diplomats and international beauties, who all seemed to have been sent over from Central Casting. Everyone danced and dined outdoors on a stage jutting out over the sea. After the Monte Carlo Ballet and fireworks, some people drifted to the tables, many to watch at the big baccarat table; where The Man Who Broke the Bank at Monte Carlo would still have felt at home.

Anyone who imagined that the age of elegance was dead had only to take a plane on an hour's flight to find it living on in sparkling freshness at Deauville. No glossier cars, bigger yachts or smarter women were to be found in Europe. The high season lasted from mid-June to the end of August. Regattas, polo matches, *concours d'élégance* crowded the summer programme, but the most important sporting events remained the race meetings. Racing enthusiasts and horse-breeders came from all over the world, particularly during the last two weeks of August, when the famous yearling sales were held at the course immediately after the races. Enchanted, leisured days were spent strolling down the boardwalk with its gaily coloured umbrellas and fluttering flags, taking an *apéritif*, stopping to watch the golden-brown children playing on the beach and the lifeguards immaculate in white duck trousers – and, of course, playing golf. At night the Casino was the perfect setting for beautiful women, their furs and their jewels.

An alternative to August in Deauville was a week at the Dublin Horse Show, of which the highlight was the international contest for the Aga Khan Trophy. 'In Horse Show Week, everything happens at once,' reported Lord Kilbracken in *Vogue*, 'an *embarras de richesse* after months of ennui'. The international set met the Irish horsey set beside the show rings, 'surrounded by brass bands and Balenciagas' or in the beflowered jumping enclosure, surrounded by Guards' moustaches and rough tweeds; or at any of the pink-coated Hunt Balls, where champagne circulated all night among the wild-eyed London debs and their chinless London escorts on their annual invasion of Dublin.

The Deauville Season: *Above*, *Vogue*'s artist, Eric, catches the tense excitement as a yearling is paraded. *Left*, at the Casino there is a fascination in the croupiers' skilful movements, and the play, often for high stakes, holds drama for players and onlookers alike ... Here Eric has drawn the baccarat table in the Salle Privée, with Miss Gloria Swanson amongst the players. *Opposite*, a typical pre-lunch scene at the well-known Bar du Soleil, with two equally well-known Deauville habitués ... bearded Van Dongen, the painter, in his characteristic red muffler, and Mr T. Simpson, who came to Deauville twenty years ago to lay out the now famous 'New Golf'. 1954.

# SOCIETY AT HOME

*Vogue* invited its readers into the private world of the international set to experience the taste and imagination which they brought to decorating their homes. Some had great works of art and grand houses, others transformed farm houses, penthouse apartments or streamlined yachts into beautiful and luxurious environments. Mr and Mrs Stavros Niarchos' various *ménages* in London, New York, Paris and on the Riviera, were like 'small museums with superb furniture and paintings'. Their penthouse at Claridges was green, white and gold, jewelled with Fabergé bibelots, Louis XVI pieces, a Savonnerie carpet, rare porcelain and canvases by Van Gogh, Cézanne, Pissarro and Renoir. 'Nearly a million pounds' worth of art goes seafaring on the eel-sleek, black, three-masted schooner *Creole* when the Niarchos are aboard,' reported *Vogue*. Two of their most valuable paintings were housed in their New York apartment – El Creco's *Pietà* and *St Peter*.

Another extravagant yacht was Mr and Mrs Arturo Lopez-Willshaw's *Gaviota IV*, which had an extraordinarily un-yachtlike interior. With its ormolu, *chinoiserie* and fine French furniture it looked more like an eighteenth-century *folie*. The Lopez-Willshaws had made their house in Neuilly, near Paris, a concise encyclopedia, illustrated, of international taste, and on the *Gaviota* each room had a special starting point. The Turkish room, with nothing Turkish actually in it, began with a small Savonnerie tapestry of a Turkish scene. The Chinese room evolved from four Chinese paintings, once in the collection of the late Duke of Kent, done by eighteenth-century missionaries; Mr Lopez-Willshaw's bedroom from four graceful gold and white Louis XVI columns.

Mr and Mrs Charles Wrightsman were great American collectors whose special prizes were a Vermeer portrait and a pair of Tiepolos. Their magnificent collection of eighteenth-century-French furniture was displayed in their ocean-front Palm Beach house, formerly the home of the legendarily chic Mrs Harrison Williams.

The difference between Christian Dior's two homes was as great as that between his tweed sports suits and his embroidered ball dresses. In his old mill house at Milly, near Fontainebleau – white walls, stone and red-tiled floors, great blackened beams. His Paris house, by contrast, was rich and elaborate, 'reflecting the times of

***Opposite,*** **Mrs William 'Babe' Paley on the parasol-roofed patio of her new house at Round Hill, Jamaica. 1956. RAWLINGS. *Above,* the *trompe-l'oeil* entrance hall at La Fiorentina, the rebuilt Palladian villa at St Jean Cap Ferrat of the Countess of Kenmare and her son, Mr Roderick Cameron. 1958. ANTHONY DENNEY.**

**The rich elaboration of Christian Dior's Paris house. *Above*, the panelled upstairs sitting room, 'a showcase for drawings by Bérard, Cocteau and La Fresnaye', and *opposite*, the exotic winter garden. 1958. ANTHONY DENNEY.**

Madame Bovary, Whistler, Louis XVI and the Augustan Empire'. Precious *objets* were everywhere – particularly Persian and early Chinese, but despite the echoes of many epochs the house had unity. Various shades of red, white and green followed through the rooms which repeated the use of textured fabrics for wall hangings and of ormolu and silver for highlights.

*Vogue* visited the New York headquarters of another great couturier, Coco Chanel, 'a small dynamo of a woman, possessed of accurate taste as some people are of perfect pitch'. Chanel lived surrounded by beige – here there were beige carpets, honey-beige straw-cloth walls, blonde-beige woods, rosy-beige leather on fine old French chairs. She also loved and collected Coromandel screens; two superb twelve-fold screens covered two walls of the reception room, while a third wall was mirror – another famous Chanel decorating trademark.

'The filtered glow of an English country house' – clear, keyed-up colours and day-long floods of sun – gave Cole Porter's New York apartment a quality of detachment from city life, although it was on the 33rd floor of the Waldorf-Astoria hotel. The graceful, curving French furniture was originally bought in the 1920s for the Porters' Paris house, which had been the scene of – among other similarly epic events – the first Charleston lessons. Billy Baldwin designed the apartment and invented free-standing bookcases made out of shimmery brass piping for the tortoiseshell leather-walled library. 'This is the Porter workroom,' reported *Vogue*, 'although the pianos, by planned paradox, are not here at all but in the drawing room since the Porter way is to write words and music straight through before the first playing'.

Cecil Beaton's seventeenth-century country home in Wiltshire, Redditch House, was like a Wren palace *en petit* set in a typical English manor garden with a nut walk, thatch-roofed cottages and impeccable yew topiary. The interior, in spite of its classic proportions, had a contemporary sense of compactness. There were paintings everywhere, from Renaissance to modern. Colour and elegance were in evidence throughout the house, particularly in the hall with its crimson velvet curtains, marble-topped William and Mary table, marble columns and Sèvres vases of *bleu-du-roi*, and in the drawing room with its bramble-coloured walls in a

flock paper and banana yellow curtains appliquéed in red in a Louis XVI Bérain design, its fine Aubusson rug and rich French furniture.

A great friend of both Billy Baldwin and Cecil Beaton was the elegant Baroness Pauline de Rothschild. The Baron and Baroness's country house, Petit Mouton, was in the centre of France's great Médoc wine country, of which Mouton-Rothschild was among the greatest vineyards. Petit Mouton was a smaller, nineteenth-century adjunct of the original house, Grand Mouton, where Baron Philippe had his office, a wine-merchant room, a museum and, below, the famous *caves*. Baroness Pauline had a great feeling for flowers, often massing red and orange dahlias, or using nasturtiums in vases made of the small horns of rams, and decorating food with flowers 'as though it were a superb still life'.

*Opposite*, two interiors of Cecil Beaton's Redditch House. *Above*, the drawing room and *below*, the hall, 'in the grand manner on a small scale'. 1950. ANTHONY DENNEY. *Above*, El Greco's 'Pietà', in the drawing room of Mr and Mrs Stavros Niarchos' New York apartment. *Below*, Gauguin's 'Horsemen on the Beach', in the main saloon of the Niarchos' yacht *Creole*. 1958. ANTHONY DENNEY.

*Above,* the marble-ized hall and the brass-bound, leather-walled library of Cole Porter's New York apartment, on the 33rd floor of the Waldorf-Astoria Hotel. 1955. KERTÈSZ. *Below,* Rousseaus against strawcloth walls, 'the colour of wrapping paper', and a Shirvan-Khilim rug in Chanel's New York headquarters. 1953. KERTÈSZ.

***Right,*** **Martin Battersby painted this panel, one of a set of twelve, to decorate a room in Sir Duff and Lady Diana Cooper's house at Chantilly, near Paris. Motifs symbolizing their interests are painted in a grisaille trophy with brilliantly coloured *trompe-l'oeil* details. This panel shows 'personal pleasures': among them, music and the theatre, represented by a programme of *Der Rosenkavalier* and masks; flying, by a Montgolfier balloon; cards and wine. 1951. ANTHONY DENNEY. *Left,* Felix Harbord conjured this fountain of glass, paper and plastic to conceal lights in a corner of a ballroom he decorated for Mrs Edward Hulton. *Below,* Oliver Messel contrived this buffet, with its swags and looped-up cloth, its alternating candelabra and plates of fruit and food, in front of a mirror which he outlined in flowers. It formed part of his decorations for a gala performance at Covent Garden. 1951. OLIVER MESSEL.**

# HAVING A BALL

'The 1950 Paris Season combined the elegance of the French tradition with the hullabaloo of a monster country fair.' There were concerts and balls of almost royal splendour in fabulous gold-and-velvet seventeenth- and eighteenth-century mansions. There were hardly enough days to accommodate all the '*nuits de –*', enough months to take care of all the '*quinzaines de –*'. It was a special anniversary year: the 250th of the Place Vendôme, the 50th of the Paris Métro, the 150th of the Council of State. There was dancing in gardens lit with the firefly glow of vigil lights, among parterres of lilies, with diamond sprays of fireworks raining overhead. Jewels were taken from their vaults and couturiers worked feverishly to finish the lavish, almost baroque evening dresses seen everywhere. The beautiful women of Paris moved about from party to party, from gala to ball, dressed with a magnificence not seen since before the war.

The 250th anniversary of Mansard's Place Vendôme called for five days and nights of celebration. Decorated shop windows edged the Place with a chain of light, and overhead huge arc lamps concentrated on the column and statue of Napoleon dressed as a Roman emperor. The square was garlanded with green leaves and draped in red velvet, the decor by Georges Geffroy. There were parties in nearly all the apartments overlooking the square. Silhouettes framed in light leaned over the balconies to watch the festivities; costumed bands from the colonies paraded and there was a night automobile show.

At the annual ball of the Count and Countess Etienne de Beaumont there was dancing in the large eighteenth-century white and gold ballroom, its walls unexpectedly covered with a gigantic Picasso mural, appropriately entitled 'The Ball'. A splendid ball at the Hôtel Lambert on the Île St Louis was patterned after another given exactly one hundred and fifty years before

***Top,*** **David Niven, Princess Grace and Prince Rainier at a Monte Carlo Ball in 1959.** ***Centre,*** **Mme Miguel Carcano, M. Yul Brynner and Mlle Doris Kleiner (later Mme Yul Brynner), at Baron Guy de Rothschild's birthday party in 1959. JACQUES VERROUST.** ***Right,*** **Miss Elizabeth Taylor at a New York party in 1951. DE MORGOLI.** ***Far right,*** **eighteen-year-old Countess Dolores von Furstenberg, dressed by Balenciaga, at a Paris party in 1955. DE MORGOLI.**

In 1957 Charles de Beistegui gave a gala performance in the newly finished private theatre at his Château de Groussay, near Paris. In the shimmering white-and-gold theatre the Comédie-Française played two comedies with sets and costumes designed by M. de Beistegui. *Above*, M. de Beistegui with Mme Jacques Pol-Roger at the head of the stairs; seated near them, Donna Anna Maria Aldobrandini (left) and Mme Arturo Lopez-Willshaw (right). 1957. DOISNEAU. *Top left*, Mrs Brooks Howe and Mrs Mellon Bruce (foreground) on the steps of The Plaza in New York. 1951. HAAS. *Left*, Three sisters at the 1950 Beaumont Ball in Paris: (left to right), Princess de Ligne, Princess d'Arenberg, Madame de la Haye Jousselin. DOISNEAU.

by the Polish Princess Czartiryski. The great court was roofed over, making one tremendous three-storey ballroom. The rooms overlooking the dance floor were turned into gilded, candle-lit *loges*, from which the guests looked down on the dancers eddying below. Princess Nilofaur of Hyderabad wore an amazing diamond feather necklace and Madame Schiaparelli a great gold-coloured chain like that of a mayor or a sommelier. Most of the dresses – with the exception of the Duchess of Windsor's, which was American and ballerina length – were made in Paris especially for this night. They were great-skirted, trailing, studded with sequins, heavily embroidered, metres wide.

Society never tired of dressing-up and throughout the decade numerous hosts requested their guests' company in various forms of fancy dress. Art was a popular theme: at the Masterpiece Ball in Chicago, guests wore costumes representing their favourite paintings or sculptures, while in Paris Vicomtesse Marie-Laure de Noailles invited her friends to pay homage to the glory of painters and writers from the Renaissance to the present day. Mme Jacques Fath looked fetching as a Lancret Harlequin, and Comtesse Maxine de la Falaise suitably regal as Catharine Howard. Most amusing of all was Marie-Laure's Music Hall jamboree – Mrs Harrison Williams made a sleek black cat, Christian Dior a jovial moustachioed *garçon* and the Comtesse de Beaumont an enigmatic Egyptian mummy swathed in gold lamé. For the Baronne de Cabrol's Circus Ball, in aid of underprivileged children, the flower of the French aristocracy rode into the ring cracking whips and performing dressage, in period costumes especially created by Dior, Givenchy and Lanvin-Castillo.

The couturiers were soon busy transforming their clients into Catherine the Great and other luminaries of the Imperial courts for the resourceful Baronne's Czarist charity spectacular on ice at the *Palais de Glace*. Prince Youssoupoff made the most dramatic *entrée* as a very convincing Ivan the Terrible. The chic summer resort of Biarritz, so near to Spain, was an appropriate setting for the dramatic Goya Ball, where the guests stood on chairs to watch Pilar Lopez, the great Spanish dancer. Hundreds of workmen toiled for days building false farmyards, triumphal arches and Temples of Love for the balletomane Marquis de Cuevas's eighteenth-century

***Above***, **Vicomtesse Jacqueline de Ribes in a head-dress devised by the Marquis de Larrain (left), with Charles de Beistegui, at a ball at the Hotel Lambert given by Baron Alexis de Redé,** ***opposite below right***, **greeting the Vicomtesse d'Harcourt. 1957. ANDRE OSTIER.** ***Opposite***, **the Hon. Mrs Reginald Fellowes, representing America, 1750, in a yellow costume by Dior, at Charles de Beistegui's Venetian masquerade ball at the Palazzo Labia. 1951. CECIL BEATON.** ***Above right***, **Nathalie Philippart, in a costume by Schiaparelli, performing the entertainment at a charity ball at the Hotel Lambert. 1950. DOISNEAU and C. P. MAGNUM.**

*fête galante* two seasons later. His own private ballet company performed a lavish entertainment. Zizi Jeanmaire made a triumphant entrance on camel-back, the Duchess of Argyll donned a halo as one of the Angels of Versailles and Merle Oberon was a shimmering vision of white and gold as a rococo version of a Greek nymph.

The party of the decade was undoubtedly the magnificent eighteenth-century Venetian masquerade ball given by the Mexican patron of the arts Charles de Beistegui in 1951. He had recently restored the famous Palazzo Labia to its former glory and he gave the ball for some 1200 friends from all over the world as a housewarming party to recreate its traditions. He also invited some 10,000 Venetians to a *fête populaire* on the piazza outside the palazzo. The firemen of Venice, in harlequin costumes, formed a pyramid like those in the great Tiepolo frescoes in the palazzo for the amusement of the guests. The palazzo had its columned courtyard hung with pale blue and gold draperies, while apparently suspended from the sky was a ten-foot chandelier of pale flowers and laurel leaves. Groups of guests entered together, forming impressive tableaux. There were eighteen *entrées*, representing everything from giants to the Court of China; all made their way to the Tiepolo room where the guests bowed elaborately to the host, who was dressed in brilliant red silk with especially built-up shoes which shot him to a towering eight feet. They then bowed to Lady Diana Cooper, in pale yellow and white as Cleopatra, standing by the Tiepolo fresco of Cleopatra and Mark Antony. Then everyone went to the courtyard to see the Cuevas Ballet, and then to dance themselves, watched by servants who wore the actual liveries of the men who served at the ball given by the Duchess of Richmond on the eve of the battle of Waterloo.

***Above right*, costumed paparazzi at the Marquis de Cuevas' eighteenth-century *fête galante* at Biarritz and, *right*, Mlle Lita Sanchez Cires and Count Guy d'Arcangues (left) as Martinique planters of the 1770s. 1953. SABINE WEISS. *Far right*, at Marie-Laure de Noailles' music hall ball: Mrs Harrison Williams as an alley-cat with Count Jacques de la Beraudière as a barman and, *opposite below left*, Christian Dior as a bistro waiter and Francis Poulenc as an illustrious old tenor. 1951. ARIK NEPO.**

At Charles de Beistegui's Venetian ball, *above*, the tableau-entrance of Lady Diana Cooper and Baron de Cabrol, as Cleopatra and Mark Antony with their suite, exactly as portrayed in the Tiepelo masterpiece in the Palazzo Labia. DOISNEAU and BEATON. *Left*, Three mystery ladies who never removed their masks; actually, they were Vicomtesse Jacqueline de Ribes, Donna Cora Caetani, and Donna Franca Antinori. 1951. DOISNEAU. *Below right*, Count Guy d'Arcangues and Count Jean d'Arcangues, in costume for the Goya Ball at Biarritz. 1953. HENRY CLARKE.

# THEATRE BOUQUETS

The early Fifties seemed to promise a revival of poetic drama in London with *Vogue* proclaiming T.S. Eliot's *The Confidential Clerk* (1953) 'the most discussed new play of the season'. In 1950 Christopher Fry was 'the most vital new talent in the theatre ... hardly known to the wider theatre public before John Gielgud produced that fascinating and irritating piece of witchery *The Lady's Not for Burning*; now we have Olivier's production of his own commission *Venus Observed*: Peter Brook's production of *Ring Round the Moon* – Fry's adaption of Anouilh's brittle little comedy *l'Invitation au Château*; and Gielgud's production of *The Boy and the Cart* ... with that admirable and deeply sincere young actor Richard Burton' – whom *Vogue* soon dubbed 'the theatre's wonder-boy'.

Peter Brook was 'the *enfant terrible* of the theatre, still only twenty-six', who 'has become almost one of its Grand Old Men, so widely is his reputation known and revered – with three productions recently running in London.' These were Nancy Mitford's adaptation of André Roussin's desert island play *The Little Hut* – 'a rather prolonged marital joke . . . which London loves'; the obscurely symbolic *A Penny for a Song* by John Whiting and *Ring Round the Moon* in which Paul Scofield played the difficult double role of the twins alongside Claire Bloom.

At the beginning of the decade, the public's favourite couples were the Oliviers – until Vivien Leigh suffered a series of nervous breakdowns – and the Lunts. Their subtlety and sophistication made successes of plays as diverse as Noel Coward's romantic comedy *Quadrille*, designed by Cecil Beaton, and Friedrich Duerrenmatt's brutally unsentimental *The Visit* in which Lynn Fontanne played the rich, icy Madame Rachanassian and Alfred Lunt her doomed seducer. Another favourite couple were Rex Harrison and Lilli Palmer, who had their chance to be enormously theatrical in a string of successes including the comedy of witchery *Bell, Book and Candle*, *The Fourposter* and the irrepressible actor/director Peter Ustinov's lively political satire *The Love of Four Colonels*. Harrison later married the 'lithe, dazzling and offbeat' Kay Kendall, who became famous for collapsing her elegant length in a variety of veteran cars in the classic Ealing comedy *Genevieve*. Her fine-boned beauty and nonchalant chic made her a favourite *Vogue* model-actress.

***Above,*** **'The scene is the Old Vic's rehearsal room, where, with a single ferocity of purpose, Hamlet and Ophelia, Richard Burton and Claire Bloom, are hammering out the Nunnery Scene under the eye of the producer, Michael Benthall. These are scenes the public never sees – just as dramatic and perhaps more important than the perfected result.' 1953. NORMAN PARKINSON. *Opposite,* Sir Laurence Olivier and Vivien Leigh as Shakespeare's *Antony and Cleopatra,* whom they played at alternating performances with Shaw's *Caesar and Cleopatra,* thus covering the most vital episodes in the loves and education of the Egyptian witch-lady. 1951. NORMAN PARKINSON.**

Terence Rattigan, 'most elegantly prolific of playwrights', retained popularity with his tautly structured drama *The Deep Blue Sea* (1952) starring Peggy Ashcroft, and his Coronation comedy *The Sleeping Prince*, which offered the irresistible combination of the Oliviers and crowned heads and chorus girls – it eventually transferred to Broadway with Michael Redgrave and on to Hollywood with Marilyn Monroe. Rattigan's double-bill *Separate Tables* (1956) ran for two seasons in London and on Broadway starring Margaret Leighton and Eric Portman; its success 'a compound of superb performances and the author's quick sympathy for battered humanity'.

Anna Massey made a double début when, just before her own coming-out dance, she became the key-charmer in *The Reluctant Débutante*. William Douglas Home's beguiling bent for satire made his funny, fork-tongued play a hit in London and on Broadway. Dorothy Tutin – 'a young actress with a robin charm and a quick attack' – became a star playing the 'young, direct and thoroughly unneurotic girl' in *The Living Room* (1954), Graham Greene's controversial Roman Catholic first play. Her Shakespearean roles as Juliet, Viola and Ophelia led *Vogue* to see her as 'the clearest Dame-material of her generation'. Indeed Shakespeare received brilliant homage throughout the decade: at Stratford under Anthony Quayle and Peter Hall; at the Old Vic under Michael Benthall and Laurence Olivier and from directors Glen Byam Shaw, Douglas Seale, Tony Richardson and Peter Brook. In Brook's Festival production of *The Winter's Tale* John Gielgud played the jealous Leontes with Diana Wynyard and Flora Robson. Gielgud also played King Lear and was a moving Angelo in Peter Brook's *Measure for Measure* at Stratford in 1950. *Antony and Cleopatra* were played by the Oliviers for the Festival and later by Michael Redgrave and Peggy Ashcroft, while Paul Scofield played Richard II and Alec Guinness Richard III. Redgrave, Scofield and Guinness all played Hamlet, as did Richard Burton; his Ophelia was Claire Bloom who also played opposite him in *Twelfth Night*. Other outstanding performers were Rachel Kempson, Irene Worth, Mary Ure and Geraldine McEwan.

*Vogue*'s favourite Dame of the English stage was Edith Evans who as the lovely alcoholic in

***Above***, **John Gielgud, 'the cynosure of the theatre', as Leontes in Peter Brook's production of *The Winter's Tale*, one of the *pièces de résistance* of the Festival's theatrical bouquet. 1951. NORMAN PARKINSON. *Opposite left*, Paul Scofield, 'an actor of rapt fidelity and ever-increasing strength'. 1951. PENN. *Top right*, Alec Guinness as the Elizabethan, anti-romantic *Hamlet* in his own production at the New Theatre, 1951. CECIL BEATON. *Below right*, Michael Redgrave as Antony in Glen Byam Shaw's Stratford production of *Antony and Cleopatra;* Peggy Ashcroft played Cleopatra. 1953. CECIL BEATON.**

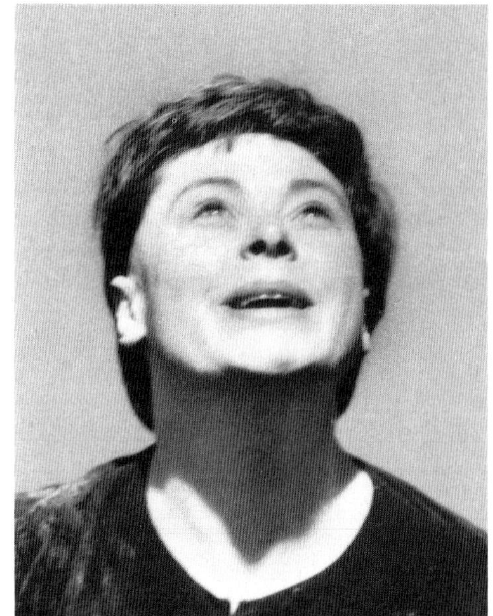

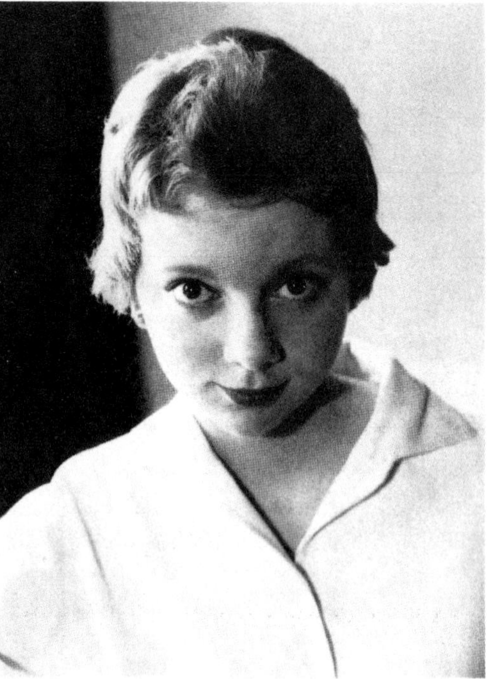

*Daphne Laureola* (1950) transformed an inconclusive play into a theatre triumph, and as the elderly lady in Enid Bagnold's *The Chalk Garden* (1956) played with rare and imperious beauty alongside Peggy Ashcroft and newcomer Siobhan McKenna. But even the combined talents of Edith Evans, Oliver Messel and Peter Brook failed to make a success of what was to be the last of Christopher Fry's quick succession of plays *The Dark is Light Enough* (1954).

For popular taste was changing and a young generation of rebellious playwrights sparked off a new wave of British drama. In 1956 John Osborne's *Look Back in Anger* with Alan Bates and Mary Ure was presented at the Royal Court Theatre. *Vogue*'s theatre critic Penelope Gilliatt proclaimed: 'The play of its decade ... (it) worked like an enema of dynamite on the polite pretence that all was fine and regular in a world of stage drawing-rooms ... Osborne shows his postwar rebels as seekers without a cause, who clutch their failures on the world's woes; find consolation in adultery, fulfilment in the self-replenishment of tears and fury.' The play's anti-hero, Jimmy Porter, reflected the disaffection of young people in the Fifties and their attack on the establishment, and caused young theatre critic Kenneth Tynan to admire the play for presenting 'postwar youth as it really is'. 'By putting the sex war and the class war onto one stage,' he declared, 'Mr Osborne gave the drama a tremendous nudge forward.'

Osborne had broken the middle-class grip on drama and opened up the stage to a new range of completely neglected anti-Establishment characters and to a new species of actors and actresses who, scorning the brittle upper-class vowels of drama school, cultivated regional and lower-class accents – Albert Finney, Peter O'Toole, Alan Bates, Kenneth Haigh, Tom Courtenay and many others. Joan Plowright played Laurence Olivier's daughter in what was perhaps Osborne's finest play, *The Entertainer* (1958), in which he cruelly parodied the decline of England through the deterioration of a seedy music-hall performer, Archie Rice. Other new 'kitchen-sink' dramas which dispensed with the need for realistic sets or elaborate costumes soon followed. They were often performed in a new type of theatre, termed 'fringe' in London or 'off-Broadway' in New York, which sprang up in areas removed from the conventional theatre

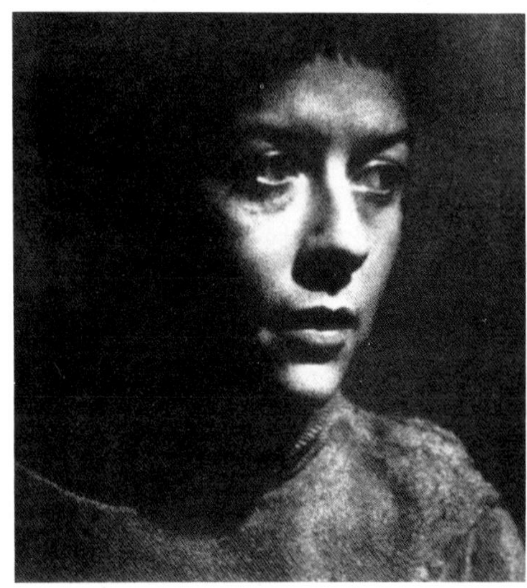

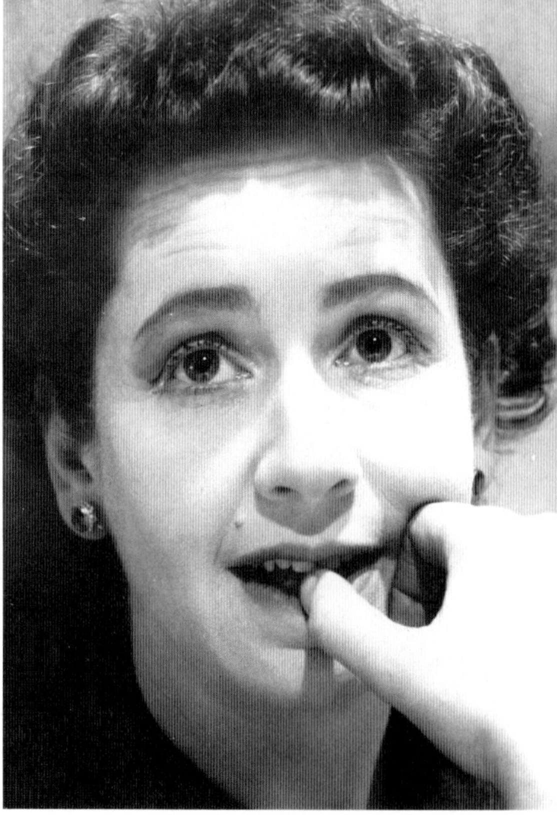

**Two young actresses played Saint Joan in 1955: *Top left*, Siobhan McKenna as Shaw's *Saint Joan* – 'It is hard to imagine a more total identification of actress and Shaw's Joan, healthy peasant girl, mystic and militant saint.' HAMMARSKIÖLD. *Above*, Dorothy Tutin as Anouilh's (and Christopher Fry's) Joan in *The Lark* – 'bird-bright, touching, very young'. HAMMARSKIÖLD. *Above right*, Anna Massey whose youth and charm illuminated *The Reluctant Debutante*. HAMMARSKIÖLD. 1950. MOSER. *Below right*, Peggy Ashcroft starred in Terence Rattigan's new play *The Deep Blue Sea* in 1952. NORMAN PARKINSON. *Opposite left*, Flora Robson and Beatrix Lehmann, together for the first time in Michael Redgrave's adaptation of Henry James's *The Aspern Papers*. 1959. ANTONY ARMSTRONG-JONES. *Opposite above right*, Mary Ure as Ophelia in Peter Brook's production of *Hamlet*. 1955. NORMAN PARKINSON. *Opposite below right*, Edith Evans, 'whose genius has attained brilliant and radiant maturity', as the feckless heroine of *Daphne Laureola*. 1950. MOSER.**

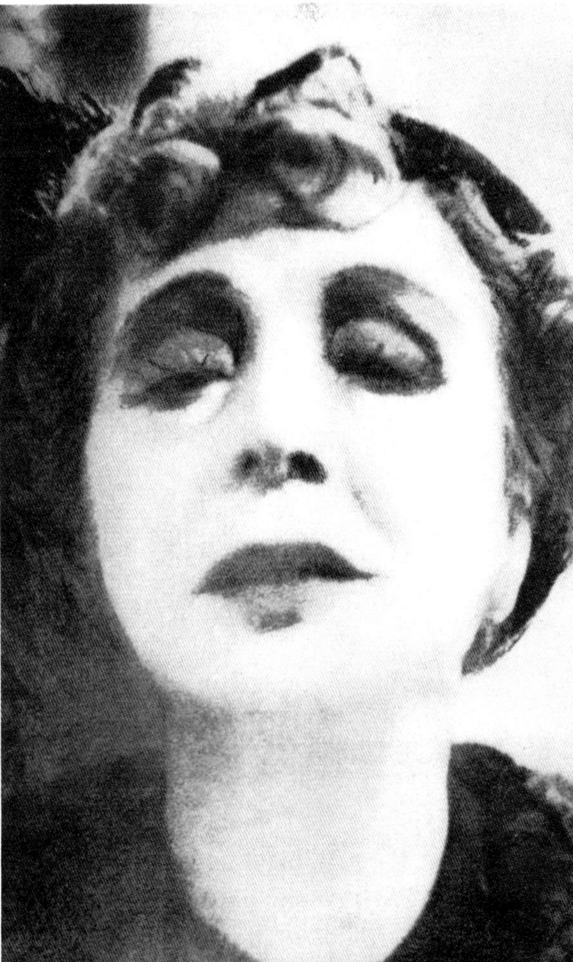

districts, where productions could afford to be controversial. George Devine's English Stage Company's policy was to encourage young dramatists who found the prevailing West End atmosphere depressing. At the Royal Court they presented Arnold Wesker's famous *Trilogy* – a quasi-epic history of two Jewish families – and John Arden's unnervingly objective parable of pacific war, *Serjeant Musgrave's Dance* (1959).

Joan Littlewood, 'a warm, forthright genius with a unique vision of theatre', presented 19-year-old Shelagh Delaney's *A Taste of Honey* (1959) – 'an incorrigible and triumphant play set in a Lancashire bedroom' – and the Irish Brendan Behan's brutal IRA prison drama *The Hostage* (1958) at her East End Theatre Workshop. Paradoxically they were so successful that they transferred to the 'alien luxe' of the West End.

Across the Atlantic Tennessee Williams – 'whose success seemed limitless' – wrote a succession of award-winning plays which wreaked havoc among the spiritual invigilators of the USA and Britain – the Boards of Censors. But *Vogue* considered: 'Tennessee Williams has acquired a reputation for violence and sex-war mongering that disregards the deep morality of his work, a centripetal love that forces his lonely characters together and insists on their communication.' In 1952 Maureen Stapleton emerged triumphant in her first great role, the wild, coarse, exalted young widow in the *Rose Tattoo*, but the verdict on *Suddenly Last Summer* (1958) was 'powerfully written, but in the end, an evanescent exercise in horror that fails: on a white hot day against a white wall on a white hill a gang of enraged children eat up a poet in search of God'. The London production of *Cat on a Hot Tin Roof* (1958) was directed by Peter Hall at the Comedy Theatre Club; *Vogue* quipped, 'No fire regulations and no censorship; in England you have to be a member to court temporal and eternal flames', and reported that American actress Kim Stanley's 'coruscant performance of Maggie, sweet and hard-centred, makes it her play'. Paul Newman was 'the sum of sex' as Chance Wayne, lost heel of *Sweet Bird of Youth* (1959), with 'the wild grace of a lynx as he bounds across the wide stage, blackmailing the equally wild Geraldine Page'.

Eugene O'Neill's autobiographical masterpiece *Long Day's Journey into Night* (1956) explored with grim, abrasive splendour his youth

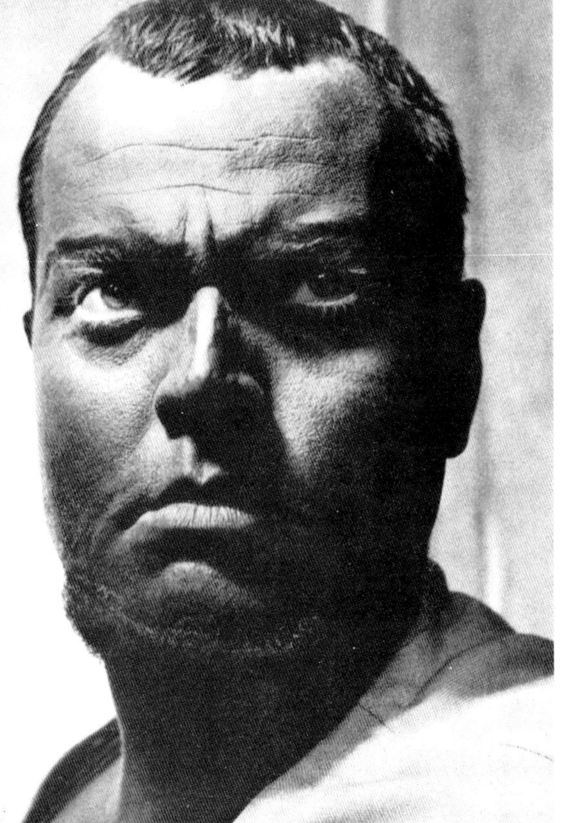

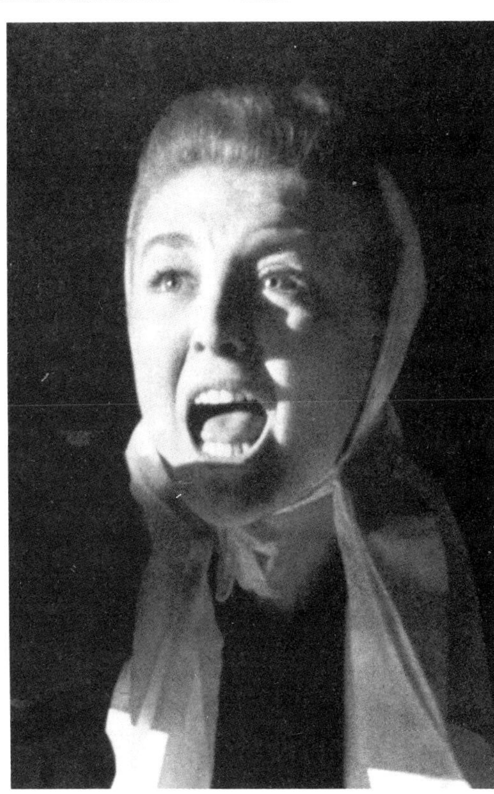

*Opposite,* Paul Newman, 'the king of the Ornamental Lug School of acting', as Chance Wayne, lost heel of *Sweet Bird of Youth.* 1959. FRIEDMAN-ABELES. *Top left,* Orson Welles, unforgettable as Shakespeare's *Othello,* of which he also made a film version. 1951. JOHN DEAKIN. *Above,* Nicole Courcel as the demonic Abigail in Arthur Miller's *The Crucible.* 1955. ROBERT DOISNEAU. *Right,* Maureen Stapleton, star of Tennessee Williams' allusive comedy *The Rose Tattoo.* 1951. PENN.

and the wormwood ties of the O'Neill family, who were played by Fredric March and Jason Robards Jr on Broadway and by Anthony Quayle, Ian Bannen and Alan Bates in London, where it towered over the rest of the West End theatre. Arthur Miller tackled controversial topics in his 'grieved and driving new play' *The Crucible* (1953). Its story of a witchhunt in seventeenth-century Salem in which justice is crushed by fear found a contemporary echo in Senator McCarthy's anti-Communist denunciations in Washington DC. His *View From the Bridge* (1955) metaphorically linked the docks of Brooklyn with the ancient world of Greek tragedy in a story of perverse familial relations resolved by violence. Mary Ure and Anthony Quayle starred in the London production, directed by Peter Brook at the Comedy Theatre Club.

Light relief was provided by Thornton Wilder's 'roughed-up comedy', *The Matchmaker* (1955) – 'a Dexedrine success' in New York, Edinburgh and London – in which Ruth Gordon 'goes stuttering through beautifully in a red wig ... assisted by two amusing young men, Alec McCowen and Arthur Hill'. The flamboyantly furred and furbelowed Rosalind Russell turned the *Auntie Mame* (1956) of Patrick Dennis's best-selling novel into ravishing flesh and blood in the 'costliest nonmusical in New York history'. Audiences were lost in admiration of her adroit manipulation of a nephew, a flutter of beaux, incense burners, a Japanese houseboy, and an inexhaustible number of chequebooks. Beatrice Lillie, playing the role in London, turned 'an erratic and sentimental strip-cartoon' into a 'consistently eccentric, sardonic and touching epic'.

In 1952 *Vogue* noted two new ingénue stars on Broadway – Julie Harris and Audrey Hepburn. Julie Harris's witty, swaggering style and rough-textured voice made her the light of *I Am a Camera*, holding the stage against all distractions. Audrey Hepburn had been abducted from chorus-dancing and Ealing comedy bit-parts in England to become Colette's *Gigi*, which she played 'with fabulous personal success'. When in 1954 she starred with Mel Ferrer, her husband to-be, in Giraudoux's *Ondine, Vogue* reported: 'This slim little person, with the winged eyebrows and Nefertiti head and throat, is the world's darling, now without rival.'

The Parisian Theatre was dominated by Jean

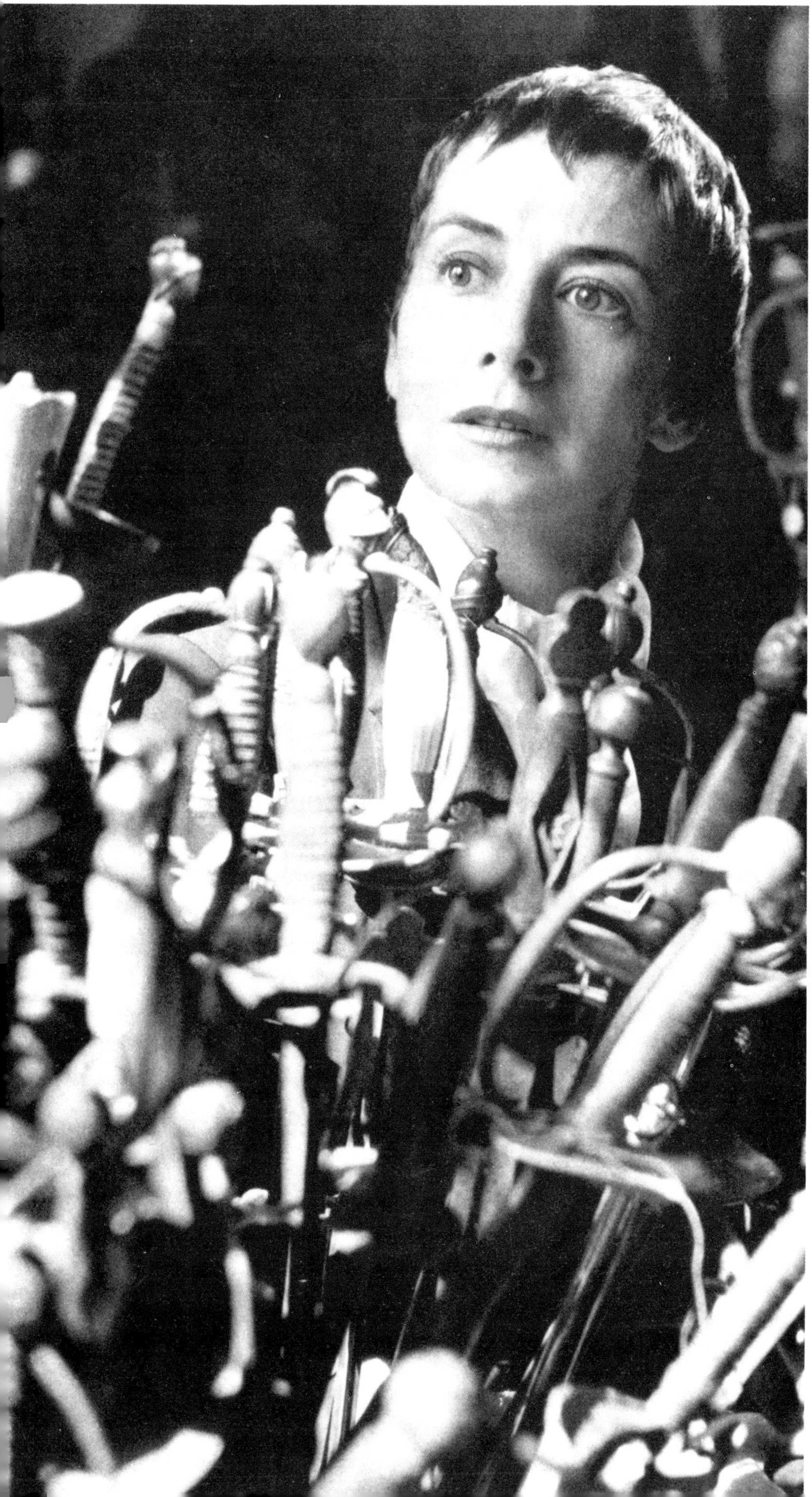

*Opposite,* Jean-Louis Barrault, 'an ascetic whose looks have the fierce nobility of a Byzantine ram', in Claudel's *Le Soulier de Satin.* 1959. WILLIAM KLEIN. *Left,* Suzanne Flon as Anouilh's Saint Joan in *l'Alouette.* 1954. ROBERT DOISNEAU. *Top,* Jean-Paul Belmondo, young star of Claude Magnier's comedy *Oscar.* 1958. ROBERT DOISNEAU. *Above,* Edwige Feuillère, photographed by Henry Clarke in the dressing room that once belonged to Sarah Bernhardt, who had incarnated Marguerite in *La Dame aux Camélias* for the public of seventy years before. 1953.

***Above,*** **Bertolt Brecht. 1956. GOERDA GOEDHART. *Top,* Friedrich Duerrenmatt, the internationally acclaimed Swiss playwright and novelist. 1959. PENN. *Above left,* Thornton Wilder, whose hit comedies included *The Skin of our Teeth* and *The Matchmaker.* 1956. PENN. *Below left,* Shelagh Delaney, the 19-year-old author of *A Taste of Honey.* 1959. NORMAN PARKINSON. *Opposite,* Tennessee Williams, 'a prized playwright' photographed by Irving Penn in 1951.**

Louis Barrault – 'the French Olivier' – and his wife Madeleine Renaud, who together produced and starred in countless plays, particularly the works of leading contemporary playwrights Paul Claudel and Jean Anouilh. *Vogue* observed that, 'bitter, biting and elegant, Anouilh's plays – *pièces roses* or *pièces noires* – can make an audience laugh and cringe simultaneously'. Suzanne Flon – 'big-eyed, fragile-boned, crop-headed' – played Anouilh's St Joan in *L'Alouette* (1954). Meanwhile the young Jeanne Moreau was hailed as a born actress playing Elisa in Jean Marias's production of Shaw's *Pygmalion* (1955), and the fascinating Edwige Feuillière as *La Dame aux Camélias,* inspired *Vogue*'s homage to her 'golden voice and perfectly controlled, calculated art', which gave her 'the ageless charm of an elegant Parisian Cleopatra'.

The avant-garde in France developed the Theatre of the Absurd, which combined with disconcerting effect an extraordinary variety of discordant elements in form and content and any number of theatrical devices. Its most influential protagonist was Eugène Ionesco whose one-act 'anti-plays', such as *The Bald Prima Donna, The Lesson* and *The Chairs*, led *Vogue* to call him: 'the most disturbing playwright in Paris [who] pulls human institutions apart with the delicate anarchy of a small boy investigating a fly to see the works; he makes us laugh at his absurd inconsequentials and then whips out a bitterly convincing truth.' England found its own master of the Absurd in Harold Pinter, whose first play *The Birthday Party* was performed at the Royal Court Theatre in 1958.

But perhaps the most important and influential plays of the Fifties were *Waiting for Godot* (1953) by Samuel Beckett, which vividly portrays the modern obsession with human isolation, and the German Bertolt Brecht's *Mother Courage and Her Children*, which employes his theory of alienation to expose war in all its cruelty, with its central formidable figure nicknamed Mother Courage. On his death in 1956 *Vogue* wrote that Brecht 'steadfastly forged the theatre of his conviction – a theatre where illusion had no part, an acting style that was not identification but stone-cold reportage. It is a decade too soon to attempt any assessment of his ultimate influence on the theatre: what we see now is a blazingly original mind at work, an opening of doors ...'

*Above,* Kenneth Tynan, astute young theatre critic of the London *Observer* – 'His thinking is often tight and burning, leading to casualties'. 1958. PENN. *Top left,* Eugene Ionesco, 'the most disturbing playwright in Paris'. 1957. ANTONY ARMSTRONG-JONES. *Bottom left,* Christopher Fry, 'the most vital new talent in the theatre' in 1950. 1951. PENN. *Right,* Jean Anouilh, the brilliant, sharp-eyed author of *The Waltz of the Toreadors* and *Antigone.* 1958. PENN. *Opposite left,* John Osborne and Tony Richardson, author and director of *Look Back in Anger,* 'the play of its decade', presented at the Royal Court Theatre in 1956. PENN. *Top right,* Brendan Behan. 1958. OSWALD JONES. *Bottom right,* Peter Brook, 26-year-old Grand Old Man of the theatre. 1951. PENN.

# ART AND ARTISTS

In 1954 *Vogue* heralded a re-birth of 'the noble art of portrait-painting', citing as two of its finest exponents Graham Sutherland and Lucian Freud. Freud's portraits, 'meticulous, strong yet delicate, revealing both the nature of the subject and that of the artist, have a truth and concentration that make them outstanding.' Sutherland's penetrating psychological studies of Somerset Maugham, Helena Rubinstein, Lord Beaverbrook and Winston Churchill did not always meet with his celebrated sitters' approval. Lady Churchill had her husband's unflattering portrait destroyed.

Still more disquieting portraits emerged from the tortured vision of Francis Bacon. His blurred, enormous paintings of ominous churchmen, strange animals and disembodied heads caused a sensation and led critics to consider him 'the finest painter working in England today'. His menacing studies of screaming Popes were inspired by Velazquez's portrait of Pope Innocent X. 'Bacon creates, like the surrealists, a macabre and nightmare world of irrationality,' wrote *Vogue*, 'but achieves greater power than the surrealists by the ambiguous nature of his presences and the almost abstract means by which they are sometimes evoked.'

No animosity was aroused by the 'modern old master' Pietro Annigoni of Florence. His portrait of the Queen, looking romantic and dashing in her garter cloak, assured him of illustrious patronage. 'I tried to show her not simply with the regal dignity of a Queen, but as she appeared to me – a beautiful young woman,' he explained.

The (literally) 'kitchen sink' realism of artists like Jack Smith, Edward Middleditch and John Bratby had the same shock value as the novels and plays of Kingsley Amis and John Osborne. Their ruthlessly 'inartistic' choice of subject matter – John Bratby's typical compositions featured vigorous nudes sitting behind breakfast tables piled with cornflake packets – gained them an immediate notoriety. In 1956 John Berger wrote a satirical conversation piece on 'The New Realists at the Venice Biennale'. '*She*: I can understand Bratby. He's wild and passionate and full of temperament and turns the breakfast table into a battlefield. I know what that means! *He*: Do you? To me he's a tragic painter. He paints everything desperately, as if for the last time. And this makes most of his pictures terribly chaotic...'.

Jacob Epstein had become 'our most eminent living sculptor', whose works, once topics of violent controversy, now looked positively traditional compared to the abstract exploration of natural forms pioneered by Henry Moore and Barbara Hepworth. *Vogue* championed the work of the young figurative sculptor Elisabeth Frink, who with Eduardo Paolozzi and the social realist painters showed at the Beaux Arts Gallery. Reg Butler, Kenneth Armitage and Lynn Chadwick turned increasingly to manmade forms, like pieces of machinery, for inspiration, and the geometrical scaffolding of Butler's prize-winning design for the monument to the *Unknown Political Prisoner* (1952) caused an outcry of incomprehension.

Abstraction attracted an increasing number of painters as the public realized that abstract painting not only looked easy to do but was actually quite easy to understand. Victor Pasmore, a founder of Euston Road neo-Impressionism, surprised his admirers by rejecting realistic description for uncompromising abstract constructivism. William Scott reduced his terrain of kitchen subjects to the barest of linear forms, like diagrams of widely-spaced saucepans and frying pans.

By 1950 Picasso and Matisse were no longer the most talked-of innovators in modern painting. The capital of the avant-garde was not Paris but New York, where war-time expatriates, including Fernand Léger, Max Ernst and Piet Mondrian, had influenced the New York School of painting and the development of abstract expressionism. Jackson Pollock's free, informal technique of dripping and smearing paint on to the canvas created a new visual language which was widely imitated. Willem de Kooning's turbulent brushwork used the grotesquely distorted figure of a woman as a recognizable image. Robert Motherwell, Clifford Still and Franz Kline painted mostly in black and white, using black masses of calligraphic brush-strokes against empty white space. *Vogue* included Kline in a section of '8 New York painters with inter-

***Opposite,*** **Francis Bacon photographed by John Deakin in 1954.** ***Above right,*** **Jacob Epstein, the American-born Grand Old Man of British sculpture. 1951. PENN.** ***Below right,*** **Graham Sutherland, 'the most eminent and widely honoured of our younger painters'. 1951. PENN.** ***Above far right,*** **John Bratby, one of London's new school of ruthless realists, with one of his 'vigorous though rather gloomy nudes'. 1955. HAMMARSKIÖLD.** ***Below,*** **Elisabeth Frink, young sculptor making rapid progress – 'her strong, very positive work has already been bought by the Tate'. JOHN SADOVY.**

national influence' (1959) and described his abstractions as 'powerful expressions of form in satisfying proportions'. *Vogue* also noted 'the hammering vitality of "The Younger Americans"' show at Frank Lloyd Wright's Guggenheim Museum – 'that luminous exquisite bubble in which the collection, including the greatest Kandinskys in the world, is framed in air and light, some brilliantly cantilevered in space.'

'*Art autre*, presumably the most vexatiously evasive title ever given to a school of painting, has suddenly become an issue that matters,' wrote Penelope Gilliatt in a feature entitled 'Why *art autre*?' (1957). The *École de Paris* artists were working in a similar direction to the American abstract expressionists and at their first London exhibition at gloomy Burlington House in 1951 were denounced as the lawless teddy-boys of art.

'Only Dubuffet and Jackson Pollock have called forth so much savage denunciation, publicity, name calling and resentment from those who dislike their paintings,' reported *Vogue*. 'Those who respond to Dubuffet find that he has enlarged their vision ... he believes that he celebrates the joy of living; that he paints the beauty that some consider ugly.'

Bernard Buffet had a spectacular success with schematic figurative paintings which interpreted the gloomier aspects of existentialist philosophy. The elegantly lean and ascetically good-looking Buffet appeared frequently in *Vogue*. Another popular and gifted painter was the tragic Nicolas de Staël, who committed suicide in 1955. His figurative paintings, simplified to the point of abstraction, had a calm beauty quite alien to the violence of the American school. But the sculptor César's penchant for soldering his creations out of scrap metal from wrecked cars was a startling comment on an obsessed consumer culture paralleled by sculptors who were working across the Atlantic.

***Above right,*** **Bernard Buffet, 'cleverest and most lauded of young French painters, has committed a cool, detached, elongated nude to canvas'. 1955. ROBERT DOISNEAU. *Right,* two masters of abstract expressionism: Jackson Pollock, with his heroic abstraction 'No. 4 – 1950', and Mark Rothko, photographed in front of his painting, 'No. 2'. 1951. BLUMENFELD.**

***Above,* Georges Braque, in the garden of his summer home at Varengeville, Normandy; and *right,* his inspiration: 'Between Varengeville's ochre cliffs, the beach, the sea – greys, blacks, greens, blues, the colour harmonies of Braque – are revealed in the northern light'. 1954. ALEXANDER LIBERMAN.**

In 1956 American *Vogue* began an extraordinary series of profiles on 'Living Masters in Art', with photographs and text by Alexander Liberman. The series, which later became part of a book, included the artists Rouault, Giacometti, Villon, Chagall, Bonnard, Vlaminck, Monet, Kandinsky and Picasso. In his first article Liberman visited Georges Braque at his summer home in Normandy. The article included the illustrations shown here and began:

'You are shut off from the outside world. You are in a world all its own, Braque's world. It is warm, the light is diffused, it is like standing in a luminous womb. The Varengeville studio of Georges Braque is an immense room with a high ceiling, every ray of light carefully softened and controlled. There is no clear glass in the windows, it is all opaque, milky glass. There is an extraordinary inner glow in this room; the traditional north light has been abandoned and the warmth of the sun penetrates the studio. The walls are white, the curtains are white, the floor is covered with a straw mat. The impression is of meticulous cleanliness and order. Everything is preconceived: each space has its allotted function in this highly organized creative factory.

'Braque has divided his studio into many areas, like the stage of the mystery dramas in the Middle Ages. Areas for engraving, for drawing and watercolour, for relaxation, and the largest one for painting. There, on several easels, are canvases in progress. The paintings look like parts of the studio and the studio looks like parts of the paintings. There is no divorce; it is a complete unity. The palette looks like the paintings, the walls look like the paintings; the objects, wherever they are, look like forms that have struck and inspired Braque's eyes. Cut out and hanging in various parts of the studio are shapes that are repeated in his canvases. One painting has a large bird; on the wall the shape of the bird is cut out in white; in another place a flower is cut out – wherever you look there are bouquets of flowers. They are small as all the spots of colour in the studio are small and they correspond to the small spot of red on his monochromatic grey palette. It seems as if his need for a visual colour stimulation is made more intense by the smallness of the stimulus. Any larger bouquets in the room are monochromatic: dried corn, dried thistles. The bouquets are like preconceived Braques with their intense composition and pointed design.

'There are numerous sources of visual inspiration in his studios. In Paris he has rubber plants, decorated Polynesian shields, Etruscan sculpture. In the country, hanging on one wall, is a large Indian rug of red and gold. Scattered around are pieces of wood, crab shells, pebbles, starfish. Although Braque has shut himself away from the outside world, he has surrounded himself with reminders of nature, carefully selected, though filtered through his mind when brought into the studio. Groups of outdoor memorabilia, like a group of starfish, pebbles and net, create harmonies which Braque can transpose into totally different still-lifes. In this way the painting of a bouquet of flowers and a jug takes on the hues brought in from the beach. On little wire stands that he has built himself stand several of his bas-reliefs, reminiscent of early Minoan work. Next to his own sculpture, lying on the table, is the big pink shell of a crab on which nature has drawn its own design. There is a consonance between the two; the artist has discovered one of the changeless rhythms of nature and transposed it into his work. This is the purpose of Braque's study of flowers, shells, stones, barks of trees, of everything that is made by God and found by man.

'Behind his easels hang movable panels of fabric painted dark brown, grey, or natural sackcloth colors. Against this monochromatic and sombre backdrop, the white accents of the paintings stand out vividly. The slightest shock of light strikes very hard against the over-all quiet. The accents of light in the paintings are like sparks. Braque says he wants his paintings to be as hard as flint, so that when struck by eye and light sparks fly. . . .'

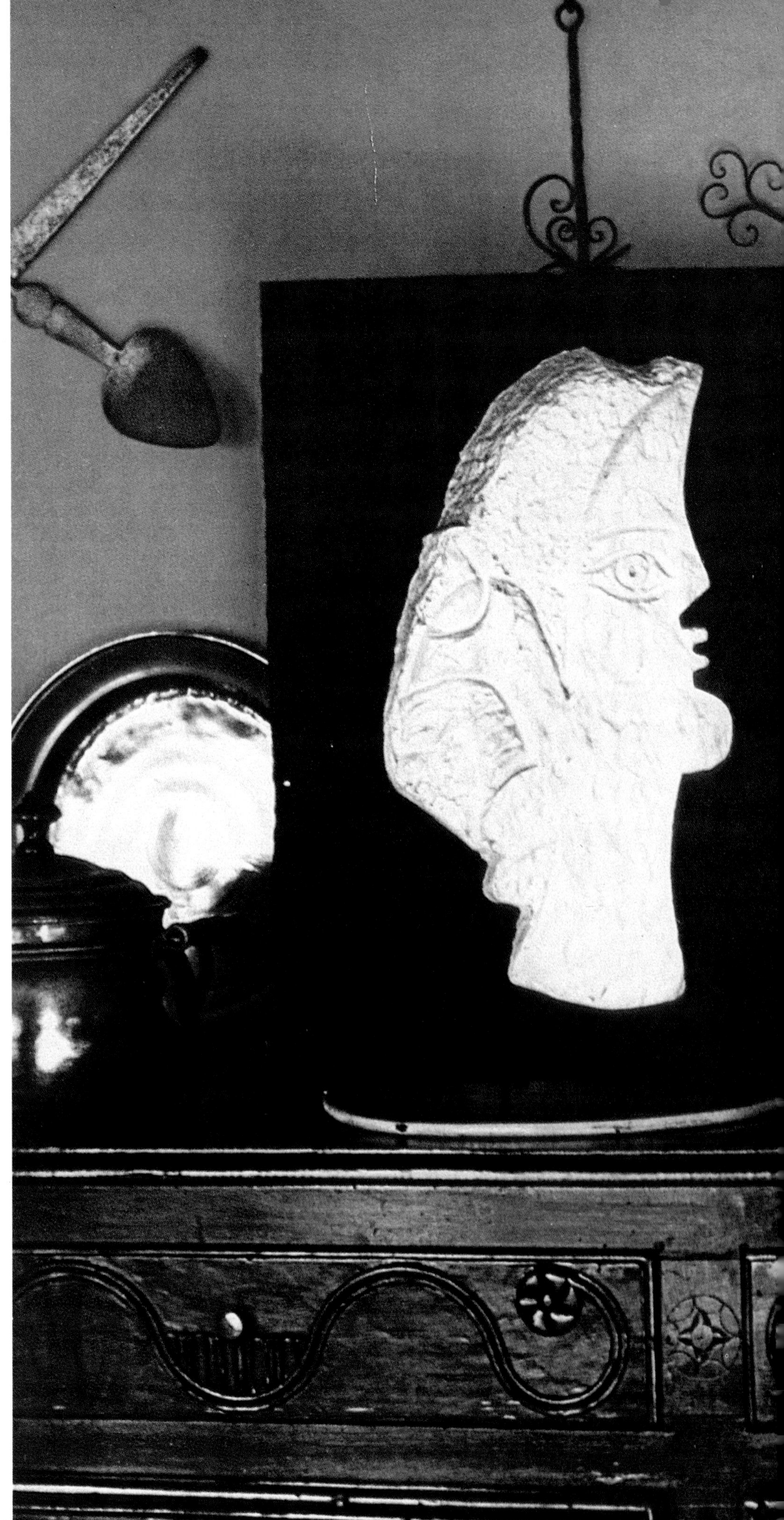

***Left***, **'In Braque's house each wall of the living-room is a different tone: ochre, yellow, orange. On an antique Norman chest stands a head, *Hesperis*, which is chiselled out of stone from the Varengeville cliffs; a pewter teapot that often appears in his lithographs; and an oil and vinegar set he made from two mineral-water bottles; on a wall, Spanish roasting forks. Intense shafts of light stream through the small windows, strike sharply the rich variety of objects and textures'. 1951. ALEXANDER LIBERMAN.**

# SONG AND DANCE

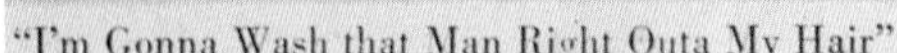

"I'm Gonna Wash that Man Right Outa My Hair"

"I'm in Love with a Wonderful Guy"

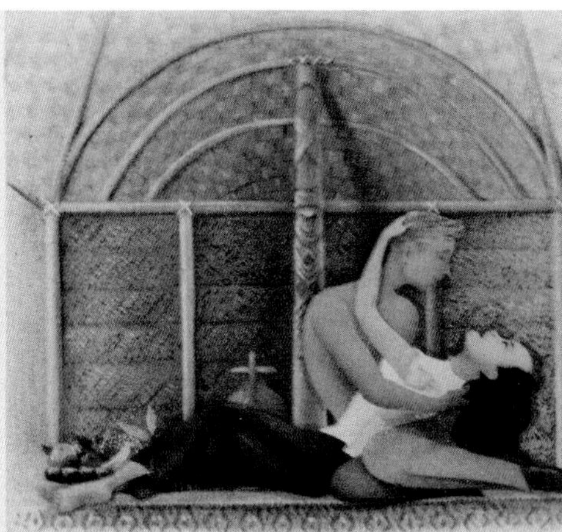

"Younger Than Springtime"

"Bloody Mary Is the Girl I Love"

"There Is Nothin' Like a Dame"

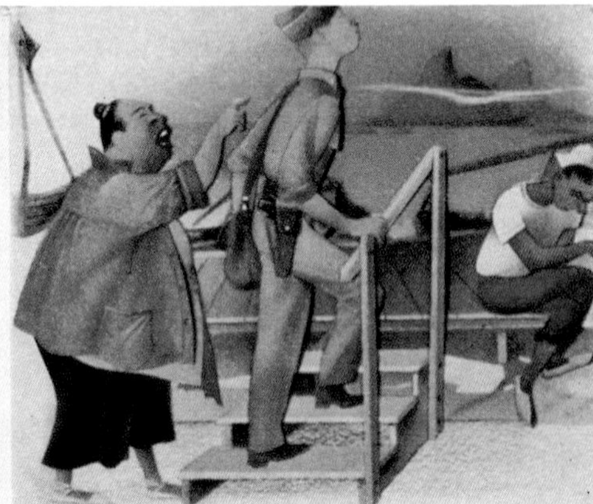

"Bali Ha'i"

"Happy Talk"

"Honey Bun"

"Some Enchanted Evening"

During the Fifties the lavish American musical, presented in bold and lively style, continued to dominate the field. Comedy was the highpoint of Frank Loesser's *Guys and Dolls* (1950), a musicalization of Damon Runyan's tough-talking sagas of New York low life, peopled with cameo characters such as Nicely-Nicely and Harry the Horse and songs as rich and strange as 'Take back your mink to from whence it came'. Another musical about the underworld was *Irma La Douce* (1958), the only long-running French musical of the decade. Penelope Gilliatt declared, 'it fuses naïveté with disbelief, the immediacy of American musicals with the French sense of déjà vu. It revels in a tough argot, but with delicate self-mockery: *Guys and Dolls* and Anouilh at a blow ... The music is indolent, offhand, and ineradicable.' As *la poule* Irma the beguiling and extravagantly toothed Elizabeth Seal sang 'Dis-donc' while tenor Keith Michell was the *mec* who fell for her proverbial heart of gold.

In contrast to such risqué urbanity, Rodgers and Hammerstein's *The King and I* (1951) was the romantic and remote tale of an English governess in nineteenth-century Siam, played by Gertrude Lawrence on Broadway and Valerie Hobson in London. It made Yul Brynner a star, 'swagger-shouldered and handsome', holding the stage against 'all the crafts and arts of Miss Lawrence ... and the enchantment of fifteen Royal Siamese children'. In Rodgers and Hammerstein's 1959 hit *The Sound of Music*, the apparently ageless Mary Martin played the strong-willed heroine Baroness Maria von Trapp who skilfully became in turn a postulant in an Austrian abbey, a bride in a Mainbocher wedding dress and a refugee escaping from the Austrian Nazis.

Irving Berlin's silky, swinging show of 1950, *Call Me Madam*, took an unabashed poke at diplomatic relations. Ethel Merman, (dressed by Mainbocher) played the lively lady ambassador Mrs Sally Adams – a gauche, good-hearted protocol-smasher. She was formidable, too, in *Gypsy* (1955), by newcomers Jules Styne and Stephen Sondheim, in which she played burlesque stripper Gipsy Rose Lee's showbusiness mother – 'a woman who alone had the push of a crowd' – and stole the show singing 'Everything's Coming Up Roses' in her rasping, electric voice. The hits of Cole Porter's *Can-Can*

***Opposite***, **scenes from Rodgers' and Hammerstein's *South Pacific*, 'a mania, a phenomenon' since its New York opening in 1949. Illustrations by Garretto. 1951. *Above*, Rex Harrison and Julie Andrews, the stars of Lerner and Loewe's *My Fair Lady*, which broke box office records around the world. 1956. CECIL BEATON.**

***Left,* Gwen Verdon in *Damn Yankees.* 1955. RENÉ BOUCHÉ. *Above,* Yul Brynner and Gertrude Lawrence in *The King and I.* 1951. GOLBY. *Opposite above,* Mary Martin, star of *South Pacific,* backstage with her son, Larry Hagman, who played one of the sailors during its London run in 1951–2. *Opposite below,* Carol Haney singing 'Steam Heat' in *The Pajama Game.* 1954. GJON MILI.**

(1953), set in Lautrec's Montmartre, were 'C'est Magnifique' and the high-kicking antics of red-headed Gwen Verdon 'cheerfully abandoning herself to break-neck dances with a sort of witty fatality'.

Verdon went on to star in shows choreographed by her husband Bob Fosse, such as *Damn Yankees* (1955) and *Redhead* (1959). Fosse's *The Pajama Game* (1954) featured Carol Haney dancing with an effect that was insanely flirtatious and simultaneously funny, singing her hit song 'Steam Heat' in a man's suit and an outsize bowler.

In England two young university graduates, Sandy Wilson and Julian Slade, produced musicals on shoestring budgets which appealed to the British public's love of amateur theatricals. Eighteen-year-old Julie Andrews was the deliciously gawky schoolgirl heroine of Sandy Wilson's *The Boyfriend* (1953). In this brilliant musical pastiche of the Twenties she sang 'in a sweet, true soprano' such endearing numbers as 'I Could be Happy with You', 'A Room in Bloomsbury' and, with the other schoolgirls immured in a correct finishing school near Nice, *We've got to have / We plot to have / For it's so dreary not to have / that certain thing called the Boyfriend.* The show – 'which everyone including Princess Margaret has seen at least once' – created a craze for the Jazz Age – the Charleston, cloche hats and expressions like 'boop-a-doop' and 'vo-de-o-do'. It became the longest running British musical with over 2000 performances. This record was soon beaten by another apparently

unambitious show, Julian Slade's sentimental and nostalgic *Salad Days* (1954). Written as a sort of 'end of term' entertainment for the Bristol Old Vic, it ended up running for five years in London's West End.

But in 1956 a new American production broke box office records around the world. Based on a British play (Shaw's *Pygmalian*) and starring British actors, *My Fair Lady* by Alan Jay Lerner with music by Frederick Loewe was undoubtedly the most successful theatrical production of the decade. It inspired a string of superlatives from *Vogue*: Julie Andrews as Cockney flower-girl Eliza Dolittle and Rex Harrison as crusty Professor Higgins were 'completely captivating', while Oliver Smith's sets 'with infinite interior jokes' and Cecil Beaton's 'wildly romantic' costumes were 'magnificently beautiful'. Everyone loved Eliza's incredulous 'Garn!' and Higgins' triumphant 'By George she's got it!'; the world was humming 'The Rain in Spain', and Beaton's memorable black and white Ascot scene created an Edwardian revival.

In 1957 *West Side Story* – 'the poetic, virile ballet with words about the Puerto Rican problem' – exploded on Broadway. In star-crossed lovers Tony and Maria of the feuding Jets and Sharks, Romeo and Juliet of the Montagues and the Capulets found a vivid contemporary counterpart. Jerome Robbins' dynamic choreography and Leonard Bernstein's tough and uningratiating music transformed the unpromising subject of juvenile gang warfare into a hit musical with a conscience.

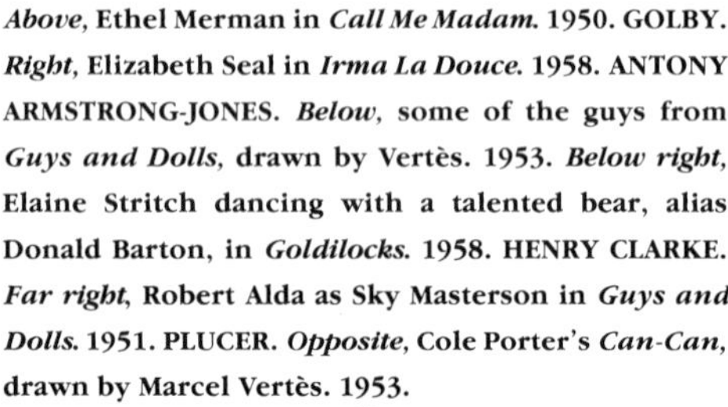

*Above,* Ethel Merman in *Call Me Madam.* 1950. GOLBY. *Right,* Elizabeth Seal in *Irma La Douce.* 1958. ANTONY ARMSTRONG-JONES. *Below,* some of the guys from *Guys and Dolls,* drawn by Vertès. 1953. *Below right,* Elaine Stritch dancing with a talented bear, alias Donald Barton, in *Goldilocks.* 1958. HENRY CLARKE. *Far right,* Robert Alda as Sky Masterson in *Guys and Dolls.* 1951. PLUCER. *Opposite,* Cole Porter's *Can-Can,* drawn by Marcel Vertès. 1953.

# ROCK 'N' JAZZ

Apart from Johnnie Ray, who sobbed out 'Little White Cloud that Cried' to an audience of screaming bobby-soxers, the early Fifties was the heyday of sentimental ballad singers like Frankie Laine and Perry Como, crooning about enchanted love in the wake of their fellow Italian-American Frank Sinatra. When Bill Haley's 'Rock Around the Clock' first exploded from the sound track of a film called *Blackboard Jungle* (1955), the teenage audience rose and jived in the aisles as if by spontaneous combustion. Rock 'n' roll, the music of youthful rebellion, had arrived. Its crude, simple, deafening vigour vibrated with a sexual energy which a husky young truck driver from Memphis soon turned into a worldwide phenomenon.

Elvis Aaron Presley didn't moon about April love in his first No. 1 hit, 'Heartbreak Hotel' (1956) – he bawled 'Ah-m-ah sah lonlah baybeh' with animal grunts and moans, manipulating his hips and guitar together in an explicitly sexual way. His brooding bad-boy good looks, deep-throated voice and gyrating pelvis had an electrifying effect upon millions of hysterical teenage girls and made him the most provocative property in show business.

Britain's answer to Elvis Presley was a succession of 'teen-dreams' of a more wholesome variety – like the toothsome Cockney charmer Tommy Steele and the earnest eighteen-year-old Cliff Richard. While Elvis was unrestrained, almost incoherent in his abandon, Cliff was, by comparison, quiet and controlled. His records and Saturday night television appearances, singing hits like 'Living Doll', were squealing successes. Just what *was* rock 'n' roll was hard to define – 'It's just the beat,' attempted Cliff, 'either you understand rock 'n' roll or you don't.' 'There is no such thing as rock 'n' roll,' announced *Vogue* in 1959. 'Reduced to crochets and quavers the beat has no hallmark of its own; the songs are of the starkest simplicity both in melody and harmony. They reach a pitch of deliberate unsophistication unique since the Stone Age.'

Jazz, adopted by the young in the Forties, now became the province of a minority that thought itself more discriminating. *Vogue* heralded the Second Jazz Age: Leonard Bernstein investigated the World of Jazz and Barry Ulanov explained that while Swing was a hot music and Bebop was less strident, the new music called

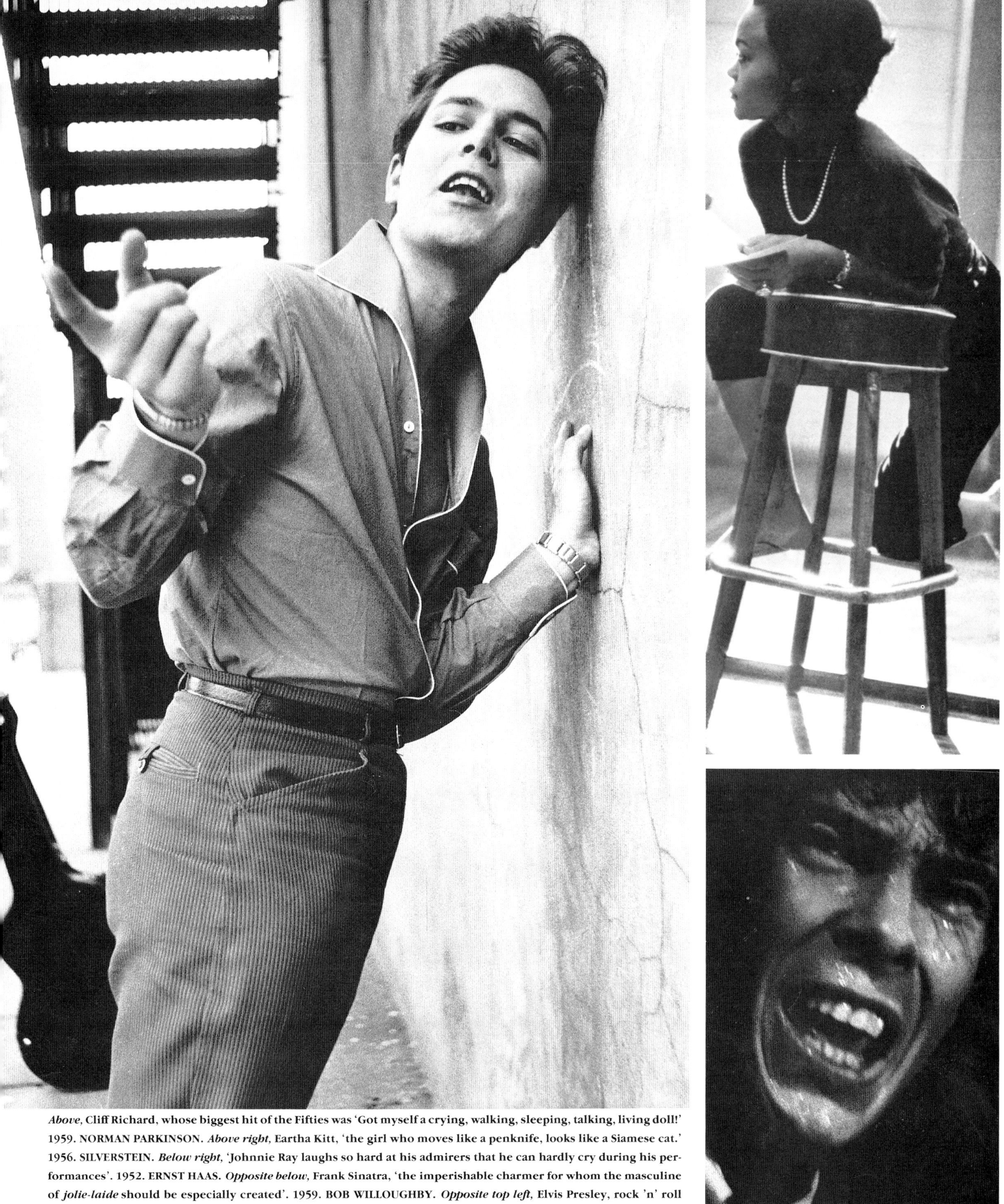

*Above*, Cliff Richard, whose biggest hit of the Fifties was 'Got myself a crying, walking, sleeping, talking, living doll!' 1959. NORMAN PARKINSON. *Above right*, Eartha Kitt, 'the girl who moves like a penknife, looks like a Siamese cat.' 1956. SILVERSTEIN. *Below right*, 'Johnnie Ray laughs so hard at his admirers that he can hardly cry during his performances'. 1952. ERNST HAAS. *Opposite below*, Frank Sinatra, 'the imperishable charmer for whom the masculine of *jolie-laide* should be especially created'. 1959. BOB WILLOUGHBY. *Opposite top left*, Elvis Presley, rock 'n' roll idol. 1959 MGM. *Opposite top right*, Tommy Steele, rock 'n' roll's boy-next-door. 1958. ANTONY ARMSTRONG-JONES.

***Above***, **Stan Kenton, the father of Progressive Jazz. 1956.** ***Above right***, **two lords of jazz together: Louis Armstrong, the trumpeter with the buried-alive voice, and Duke Ellington, six-foot one of sweet-talking langour. 1955. PENN.** ***Below***, **the composer-pianist, Dave Brubeck, high-priest of Cool Jazz.** ***Right***, **Stan Getz, tenor saxophonist: internationally imitated, moved from Dixieland Jazz to Cool. 1952. PENN.**

'Cool' was more restrained than the jazz of the past and its musicians more aware of the depth and breadth of jazz. Cool was the hallmark of the piano playing of Lennie Tristano and Dave Brubeck, of the alto-saxophone as Charlie Parker and Lee Konitz played it, of John LaPorta's clarinet playing and of the tenor saxophone solos of Stan Getz and Lester Young.

The High Priests of Cool Jazz were the composer–pianists John Lewis, formerly of Dizzy Gillespie's Bebop band, who founded the ultra-cerebral Modern Jazz Quartet, and Dave Brubeck, a pupil of Darius Milhaud, whose record 'Take Five' was a hit which broke through to the non-specialist audience. The characteristic austerity of Cool soon created a counter-revival of New Orleans Trad Jazz on both sides of the Atlantic. Old Etonian Humph Lyttleton led a devoted following to his club at 100 Oxford Street and bandleaders Ken Colyer and Chris Barber paved the way for a Trad boom of showbiz jazzmen like the clarinet-playing, bowler-hatted Mister Acker Bilk.

*Above,* Lester Young, tenor sax (left) with Charlie 'Bird' Parker, the alto saxophonist whose free-swinging cadenzas liberated the jazz soloist. 1952. PENN. *Top left,* Charlie Mingus, the great bass player. 1955. PENN. *Left,* trumpeter Humphrey Lyttelton. 1955. NORMAN PARKINSON.

# THE BIG SCREEN

Hollywood's chief rival was now television; on both sides of the Atlantic people would no longer go out to see what they could see for nothing at home. The studios found they must produce what television did not – either huge spectacles or smaller, more intelligent films which no longer had to have sentimental happy endings. Two bitterly realistic films of 1950 were Billy Wilder's brilliant *Sunset Boulevard* and Joseph Mankiewicz's *All About Eve*. In the former, Gloria Swanson played a larger-than-life silent-screen idol who, dreaming of a come-back, ultimately descends into murder and madness; and in the latter the indomitable Bette Davis, as a leading actress usurped by a scheming newcomer, perfected the art of understatement, saying it all in the flicker of an eyelid.

During the five years after commercial television started in Britain in 1955, cinema audiences halved.

Hollywood's reaction to television's small screen was to counter-attack with a bigger and better one to lure the public back to the box office. Each successive wonder of wide-screen, new colour processes and stereophonic sound – Cinerama (1952), Cinemascope (1953), Vista-vision (1954) and Todd-AO (1956) – was hailed as 'the most important motion-picture milestone in twenty years'. In the travelogue *This is Cinerama* (1952) three projectors trained on a huge curved screen produced a nearly 3-D effect which, combined with omnidirectional microphones, surrounded the audience in action and sound. 'Even wiseacre hearts swivel during the roller-coaster sequence, nostalgic travellers breathe the ripeness of Venetian canals, and even non-chauvinistic heckles rise to the sweep of America'. *How to Marry a Millionaire* (1953) featured Marilyn Monroe 'burbling to Lauren Bacall about money across acres of screen',

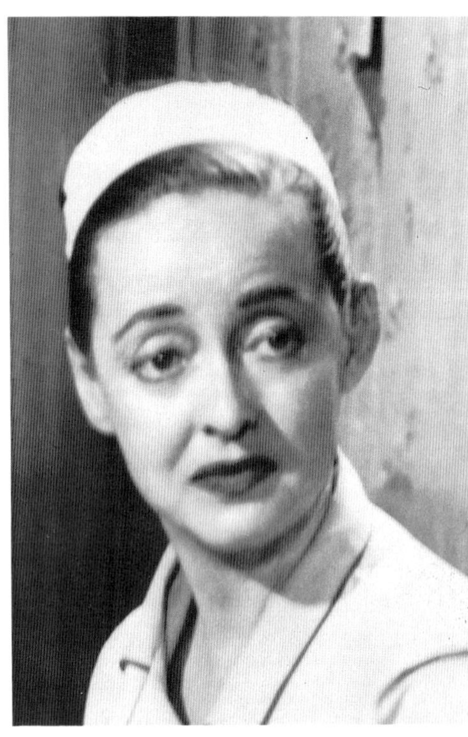

***Above left,*** **Bette Davis, 'just about the best actress in the movies', who had just won an Academy Award for her role in *All About Eve*, 1950. *Above right*, Jayne Mansfield, Hollywood's Queen of the erogenous zones. Her breasts were insured for a million dollars. 1950. *Right*, Marilyn Monroe, 'like a ripe, sleepy fruit dangled just out of teeth reach', in *The Prince and the Showgirl* with Laurence Olivier. 1956. MILTON GREEN. *Far right*, Gina Lollobrigida. The Italian screen bombshell made her first appearance in English in John Huston's *Beat the Devil*, 1953. DEAKIN.**

while Walt Disney's astonishing nature films like *Secrets of Life* and *The Living Desert* (1954) 'put human actors out of business'. Diaghilev-like impresario Mike Todd developed Todd-AO for his multi-million-dollar, all-star 'epic of resourcefulness', Jules Verne's *Around the World in Eighty Days* (1956) in which David Niven played Phineas Fogg.

But nothing could diminish the appeal of television and in 1955 even Hollywood started to produce tele-films, churning out a glut of mini-Westerns which became the staple diet of television viewers all over the Western world. Television writers like Paddy Chayevsky also made their contribution to cinema by bringing contemporary stories about ordinary people to the big screen with successes like *Marty* (1955) and *The Bachelor Party* (1957). A spate of new-style films by television-influenced directors followed: gripping anecdotes like Sidney Lumet's *Twelve Angry Men* (1957) and satirical essays like Alexander Mackendrick's *Sweet Smell of Success* (1957) with Burt Lancaster and Tony Curtis.

Until 1956 Hollywood's creativity was severely inhibited by McCarthyism – the UnAmerican Activities Committee hearings, the Black Lists and the consequent exodus of talents to Europe. Any hint of social criticism was dangerous and a non-controversial conformity prevailed. One irreproachable genre was the Biblical epic, its sincerity attested to by the amount of money spent on it. 'In producing *Quo Vadis*' (1952), announced a spokesman, 'MGM has performed an act of faith.' Peter Ustinov headed a cast of 30,000 as 'a rather cuddly and very frightened Nero': *Vogue* noted the audience's anxiety to get to the lions and pronounced the spectacle 'about as debauched as a split banana'.

While Fox Cinemascoped the religious splendours and miseries of *The Robe* (1953) with Jean Simmons, Cecil B. de Mille parted the Red Sea in Panavision for Paramount's *The Ten Commandments* (1953) – which bosomy Jayne Mansfield claimed she lived up to 'one hundred per cent'. *Vogue* dismissed it as 'full of fake celestial thunder-bolts and wretched acting, except for Edward G. Robinson as a rich, self-made heel and Yul Brynner, splendidly barbaric as Rameses'. Brynner also starred in *Solomon and Sheba* (1959) with the voluptuous Gina Lollobrigida and 'an uncredited actor as the voice of God, which by the miracle of Super Technorama

***Above***, **Gloria Swanson, legendary silent-screen star of over sixty films, returned to star in *Sunset Boulevard*, and heard again Cecil B. DeMille's magical direction: 'Lights, camera, action, close-up'. 1950. PENN.**

***Top,* Jean Seberg, the girl from Iowa picked by Otto Preminger to play *Saint Joan,* 1957. NORMAN PARKINSON. *Above,* the impish Shirley Maclaine, Hollywood's favourite young comedienne. 1959. *Right,* Leslie Caron, the world's Cinderella, star of *The Glass Slipper,* 1954. JEAN HOWARD. *Opposite,* Audrey Hepburn, who created a new ideal of beauty, 1954. CECIL BEATON.**

issues celestially from a spot over the Gents'. The most colossal epic of them all was the multi-Oscar-winning *Ben-Hur* (1959), MGM's remake of a silent movie which even the talents of several successive writers including Gore Vidal and Christopher Fry failed to make interesting.

When Hollywood was not persecuting early Christians or Jews on a lavish scale it still found time for big screen Westerns, like Fred Zinnemann's brilliant allegory on McCarthyism, *High Noon* (1952), starring Gary Cooper. Another favourite theme was the steppe-sized historical epic like *War and Peace* (1956), which lost the rich complexity of Tolstoy and became 'in spite of the flames of visual glory and the triumphs of haberdashery and dressmaking, probably the least Russian movie ever made'. The variously accented cast included Henry Fonda, Herbert Lom as Napoleon, John Mills, Audrey Hepburn and Mel Ferrer, and Swedish blonde Anita Ekberg as the Princess Elena Kouraguine – 'an invention of Tolstoy's that anticipated central heating'. *Vogue* dismissed *The Pride and the Passion* (1957) as 'a Spanish *War and Peace* without genius and snow' and *The Vikings* (1958) as 'awful but entertaining . . . at the end, a one-eyed Kirk Douglas, killed by a one-armed Tony Curtis, is given a Viking's funeral and sent into the sunset on a flaming ship – Douglas *flambé*'.

Fred Zinnemann also directed the Todd-AO version of *Oklahoma!*, one of a spate of musical films – *South Pacific, Pal Joey, The King and I, Carmen Jones* – which endeavoured to reproduce the success of outstanding stage productions. Gene Kelly's freshly inventive choreography and dancing made hits of *On The Town* (1950) with Frank Sinatra, *Singin' in the Rain* (1952), an inspired remake in which Kelly danced 'You were Meant for Me' with pretty Debbie Reynolds, and *Three Coins in a Fountain* (1954). Gamine Parisian ballet dancer Leslie Caron starred in his *An American in Paris* (1953) and in the enchanting *Lili* (1954) with Mel Ferrer. *Vogue* found Caron's childlike charm and unconventional prettiness, 'rather like that of a pixie with a Sorbonne degree', irresistible. But despite her radiant sparkle in Lerner, Loewe and Beaton's *Gigi* (1959), with 'The Night They Invented Champagne' and Maurice Chevalier singing 'Thank Heaven for Little Girls' 'with a slide like a trombone', Penelope Gilliatt felt as though the film was selling something subliminally –

'MGM good evenings start with Colette'.

In *Daddy-Long-Legs* (1955) Caron partnered old-timer Fred Astaire, who had danced with agility and grace all over the furniture in *The Band Wagon* (1953) as well as 'Dancing in the Dark' with Cyd Charisse. In *Funny Face* (1957) Astaire played an Avedon-like photographer whose triumphant find, a funny face worth a fortune, was the elegant and ethereal Audrey Hepburn. A Diana Vreeland-like editor pronouncing 'Think Pink' and Astaire and Kay Thompson swinging from chandeliers and singing 'Ring Dem Bells' were highlights of this delicious fairy tale about fashion magazines. Judy Garland made a triumphant comeback in *A Star is Born* (1953), George Cukor's lavish remake of the old show-must-go-on tearjerker, with James Mason co-starring as the alcoholic actor on the skids.

Another former child star, Elizabeth Taylor, came of age playing a brittle society girl in George Steven's *A Place in the Sun* (1951) with Montgomery Clift, then went on to look 'like a rich man's wife should' in *Giant* (1954) with Rock Hudson and James Dean. In Tennessee Williams' *Suddenly Last Summer* (1959) she played the disturbed Catherine, helped by psychiatrist Montgomery Clift and terrorized by Katharine Hepburn who took the part of the autocratic and deranged Mrs Violet Venable.

Hepburn gave another memorable performance in John Huston's *African Queen* (1951), sparring with Humphrey Bogart and navigating a tin-pot craft down the dizzy rapids of an African river. Africa and Bogey also accompanied a new screen goddess, the 'dark, disturbing, panther-beauty' Ava Gardner. She went big-game hunting with a happily middle-aged Clark Gable in *Mogambo* (1953) and was herself head-hunted by a bloodshot Bogart in Joseph Mankiewicz's bitter Hollywood morality tale, *The Barefoot Contessa* (1954). Bogart was already suffering from cancer when he movingly played the lonely, paranoid and disastrous Captain Queeg in *The Caine Mutiny* (1954).

The new order of Hollywood heart-throb was christened by *Vogue* the 'masculine brute rebellion'. In 'the broad shoulders, the slouch, the regional accents, and the beautiful broad peasant features of Richard Burton,' wrote Siriol Hugh Jones, 'the inescapable animal bulk of Marlon Brando, the neurotic-baker-boy puzzle-

*Opposite,* Sophia Loren, famous as a torrent of movie sex, looking 'like a dip of coffee ice cream, cool, beautiful, and soothing'. 1958. HENRY CLARKE. *Top,* Ava Gardner, 'the world's current golden Aphrodite, piquantly spiced with the healthy handsomeness of the New World'. 1954. NORMAN PARKINSON. *Above,* Elizabeth Taylor's violet-eyed, black-and-white beauty captured by Cecil Beaton in 1954. *Right,* Grace Kelly, the snow princess, photographed by Howell Conant in 1956, the year she married Prince Rainier.

ment of Montgomery Clift, the sulking pout of Farley Granger – there lies glamour, there lies the heroic touch'. She observed that the hallmark of the new hero was stamped along his hairline – 'the postwar look is that of the crew-cut and its dire derivations'.

Marlon Brando's relaxed and neurotic Method Acting made him an actor of furious directness. His meteoric film career began with Zinnemann's *The Men* (1950) but he reached world-wide fame starring with Vivien Leigh in Elia Kazan's film of *A Streetcar Named Desire* (1952). Repeating 'the violence, the mumble, the shouting, the passion, and the shirtless biceps' that made his stage performance of Stanley Kowalski memorable, he led a troupe of younger actors into imitating his torn shirt and sullen body-building acting. He also gave volcanic performances as a motor-cycle hooligan in *The Wild One* (1954) and as a dockworker in *On the Waterfront* (1954) with Eva Marie Saint.

In 1955 *Vogue* heralded a new School-of-Brando rebel, James Dean, who slouched 'graceful as a young beast' in Steinbeck's Cain and Abel drama *East of Eden*. In all three films of Dean's brief career he played vulnerable and restless loners rebelling against the adult world. When *Rebel Without a Cause* was released two weeks after Dean's tragic death-crash en route to a motor-race meeting, *Vogue* noted the sad relevance of the plot to Dean's own life and death. But he lived on as the off-beat generation's cult-hero long after his death.

Other new-style heroes were the lanky and charm-filled Anthony Perkins and the dazzlingly handsome Paul Newman. Newman gave a 'guarded, vivid, daunting' performance in *The Long Hot Summer* (1958) – 'a film a long, hot way after Faulkner ... with an impersonation of a sperm-whale from Orson Welles'.

The Fifties heroine often depended on a child-like appeal, whether the doe-eyed alertness of Leslie Caron and Audrey Hepburn or the provocative babytalk of a succession of curvaceous blondes, whose ravishing prototype was Marilyn Monroe. Hepburn partnered Hollywood's established leading men in stylish romantic comedies like *Roman Holiday* (1953) with Gregory Peck, and *Sabrina* (1954) with Humphrey Bogart. Monroe had first attracted attention as the kittenish moll in John Huston's underworld drama *The Asphalt Jungle* (1950), but as Anita

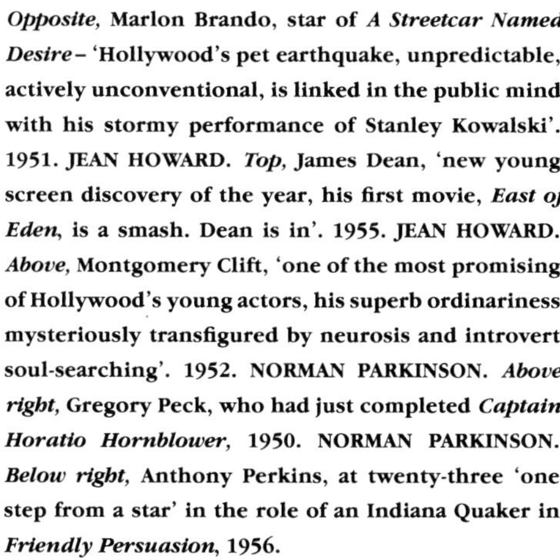

***Opposite,* Marlon Brando, star of *A Streetcar Named Desire* – 'Hollywood's pet earthquake, unpredictable, actively unconventional, is linked in the public mind with his stormy performance of Stanley Kowalski'. 1951. JEAN HOWARD. *Top,* James Dean, 'new young screen discovery of the year, his first movie, *East of Eden,* is a smash. Dean is in'. 1955. JEAN HOWARD. *Above,* Montgomery Clift, 'one of the most promising of Hollywood's young actors, his superb ordinariness mysteriously transfigured by neurosis and introvert soul-searching'. 1952. NORMAN PARKINSON. *Above right,* Gregory Peck, who had just completed *Captain Horatio Hornblower,* 1950. NORMAN PARKINSON. *Below right,* Anthony Perkins, at twenty-three 'one step from a star' in the role of an Indiana Quaker in *Friendly Persuasion,* 1956.**

Loos' gold-digging Lorelei Lee she proved she could do more than 'switch her rear and wiggle her mouth', singing 'I'm just a Little Girl from Little Rock' in *Gentlemen Prefer Blondes* (1953). She revealed an innate gift for comedy and pathos in a string of hits, including William Inge's *Bus Stop* (1956), George Axelrod's *The Seven Year Itch* (1955) and Billy Wilder's brilliantly slapstick *Some Like it Hot* (1959). The cult of the baby blonde and the popularity of shortie nighties peaked when Carroll Baker played the provocative thumb-sucking child-wife in Tennessee Williams' *Baby Doll* (1956).

The ladylike Grace Kelly was a different type of Hollywood blonde. Her gentle, fine-bred prettiness proved an unexpected box-office goldmine during a brief career. Her fragile perfection was well displayed playing haughty society girls – in Alfred Hitchcock's *To Catch a Thief* (1955), in which she chased around the Riviera with Cary Grant, 'she so ko-ool and he so seductive as a suspected cat burglar', and the following year in Cole Porter's *High Society*. In her last film *The Swan* (1956) she played a fairy tale Princess who marries a Crown Prince (Alec Guinness). It was released as she married Prince Rainier and left Hollywood for Monaco.

Master of suspense Alfred Hitchcock kept audiences on the edge of their seats with thrillers like *I Confess* (1953) with Montgomery Clift and *North by Northwest* (1959), a spy adventure pairing debonair Cary Grant with Eva Marie Saint as a 'slinky, cello-voiced vamp'. *Vertigo* (1958) starred Kim Novak, whose 'snow-flake loveliness' had its own excitement. She was groomed by Columbia as 'an ice-sculpted swan' to carry the caviar roles previously played by Grace Kelly. And in *The Trouble with Harry* (1955) Hitchcock introduced 'the best new comedienne since Marilyn Monroe . . . the dead-eyed and decorous' Shirley Maclaine.

In Britain the film industry was at a low ebb. The Ealing Studios and the Rank Organization were also having to compete with the growing power of television. Ealing Studios were sold to television in 1956 but prior to this continued to produce classic dramas like *The Blue Lamp* (1950) with Dirk Bogarde and comedies like *The Ladykillers* (1955), starring Alec Guinness as a master criminal adept at disguises, and *The Lavender Hill Mob* (1951) with Alistair Sim. Peter Sellers became famous as Guinness's co-star and

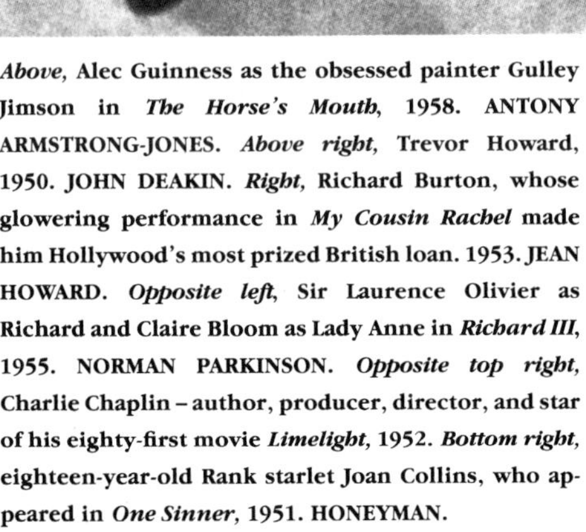

***Above,*** **Alec Guinness as the obsessed painter Gulley Jimson in *The Horse's Mouth*, 1958. ANTONY ARMSTRONG-JONES. *Above right,* Trevor Howard, 1950. JOHN DEAKIN. *Right,* Richard Burton, whose glowering performance in *My Cousin Rachel* made him Hollywood's most prized British loan. 1953. JEAN HOWARD. *Opposite left,* Sir Laurence Olivier as Richard and Claire Bloom as Lady Anne in *Richard III*, 1955. NORMAN PARKINSON. *Opposite top right,* Charlie Chaplin – author, producer, director, and star of his eighty-first movie *Limelight*, 1952. *Bottom right,* eighteen-year-old Rank starlet Joan Collins, who appeared in *One Sinner*, 1951. HONEYMAN.**

was one of a new team of comedians who flooded onto the screen, including Ian Carmichael, Terry Thomas, Dora Bryan, and Frankie Howerd. Rank also produced a first-rate comedy in *Genevieve* (1953), a witty joy-ride set in the London-to-Brighton veteran car rally, with Dinah Sheridan, Kenneth More and Kay Kendall.

The prolific Charlie Chaplin, a victim of McCarthyism and exiled from Hollywood, wrote, produced, directed and starred in his eighty-first movie *Limelight* (1952). He discovered a young dancer of fragile beauty, Claire Bloom, to co-star in his story of dedicated music-hall performers. Chaplin played, with a brilliant mix of poignancy and slapstick, a once-great comedian, now dissipated and down-at-heel, who for one wonderful evening becomes again the cane-twirling, straw-hatted Calvero, the wide-grinning clown. Claire Bloom went on to play Lady Anne in Laurence Olivier's magnificent film of *Richard III* (1956), 'a sweep of ripe colour and high-handed performances', including Ralph Richardson as a cool, devious Buckingham and Olivier as Richard, 'dying an unseemly death, bloody and quivering on a Vista-Vision screen'.

Sir Carol Reed, 'the Deity who must always go one better than *The Third Man*', directed James Mason as the hero of his subtle thriller *The Man Between* (1953) with Claire Bloom as the innocent Suzanne lost in the wilderness of contemporary Berlin. In Reed's film of Conrad's *Outcast of the Islands* (1952) Trevor Howard acted 'like a man possessed', and in his circus film *Trapeze* (1955) ex-acrobat Burt Lancaster felt at home on the high-wire with the gorgeous Gina Lollobrigida.

The versatile Alec Guinness gave outstanding performances as the obsessed painter Gully Jimson in his adaptation of Joyce Cary's *The Horse's Mouth* (1958) and as the fanatical British colonel in David Lean's *Bridge on The River Kwai* (1957). The British cinema often harked back to Second World War subjects in films like *The Cruel Sea* (1953) and *The Divided Heart* (1954).

Towards the end of the decade kitchen-sink realism entered the cinema with films like the abrasive and observant *Woman in a Dressing Gown* (1957), which was enhanced by Yvonne Mitchell's snow-and-ebony beauty. Lindsay Anderson and Karel Reisz were already making short, socially-conscious documentaries on a shoestring 'with great directness and no heavy breathing'. But two feature films of 1959, both

set in the grey industrial Midlands, signified a renaissance in British cinema. Penelope Gilliatt applauded Tony Richardson's fierce and melancholic film of John Osborne's *Look Back in Anger* as 'a rousing triumph'. She praised Jack Clayton's film of John Braine's novel *Room at the Top* for its honest portrayal of anti-hero Laurence Harvey's climb up the class ladder; and for the unheightened truth of the camerawork – 'it states what a Northern town is like: cobbled streets, smudged views of chimneys, women cooking at ranges, wet slabs of washing to be dodged by children playing in the street. I know that remarking on this is like applauding a dress for being sufficiently in touch with reality to have a zip, but it is notable in our cinema.'

In France Gérard Philipe, pale, sensitive and limpid-eyed, was everyone's favourite romantic lead. He starred in René Clair's comic version of the Faust legend *La Beauté du Diable* (1950) and in Clair's *Belles de Nuit* (1952), and became amorously entangled in many films including Ophuls' *La Ronde* (1950) and *Les Liaisons Dangereuses* (1959). Jean Renoir continued to enchant with lyrical films like his spellbinding documentary about India, *The River*, and his exquisite Italian Commedia dell'Arte comedy *The Golden Coach* (both in 1952). Mel Ferrer and Ingrid Bergman starred in his period romance *Eléna et les Hommes* (1956), while in *French Can-Can* (1955) music-hall stars like Edith Piaf and Patachou relived the glories of the Moulin Rouge and Renoir painstakingly reconstructed Bel Époque Paris 'as though Pissarro, Monet, Auguste Renoir and Lautrec had been his team of art directors'.

Another director full of *fin de siècle* nostalgia was the Austrian Max Ophuls. His *La Ronde* (1950), based on a Schnitzler play, was a pretty, witty, episodic satire on love and infidelity which enjoyed great international success. The bewitching Daniele Darrieux was *Madame de* (1953) in Ophuls' adaptation of Louise de Vilmorin's novel, with Charles Boyer and Vittorio de Sica. Martine Carol was the star of Ophuls' masterpiece *Lola Montez* (1955), a richly rococo impression of the great courtesan's career which culminated in the downfall of Ludwig I of Bavaria.

Another classic was the poetic and surreal *Orphée* (1950), the perennial *enfant terrible* Jean Cocteau's exploration of the problem of free will. A frozen-hearted and haunted Jean Marais

*Opposite,* Brigitte Bardot – William Klein photographed 'the sensuous idol' for *Vogue* in 1958, two years after *And God Created Woman* made her an international star. *Above left,* Michèle Morgan, who first gave the raincoat glamour in *Quai des brumes* (1938), photographed by Norman Parkinson in 1953. *Above right,* Danièle Delorme, wistful heroine of Colette's *Gigi* (1950) and *L'Ingénue Libertine,* 1950. ROBERT RANDALL. *Below right,* Jeanne Moreau; the seductive gangster's *poule* in Simenon's *Touchez Pas au Grisbi!* became the new love of French moviegoers, 1955. SABINE WEISS. *Far right above,* Anouk Aimée, photographed by William Klein in 1957. *Far right below,* Gérard Philipe, France's most popular leading man. 1952. COFFIN.

was the centre of 'a beautiful pattern of symbols, a series of visual images of extraordinary beauty, and ... a cold and indefinable terror that is without bounds, colour, hope or reason'. A contrast to such lush imagery was the elusive and austere work of Robert Bresson whose films included *Le Journal d'un Curé de Campagne* (1950) and *Un Condamné à Mort s'est Échappé* (1956). *Vogue* called Bresson 'the true ascetic of the screen, who uses the language of images to transcribe the secret vocabulary of the conscience'. A more approachable poet of the human comedy was the inimitable Jacques Tati whose gift for mime overstepped all language barriers. He introduced Monsieur Hulot in two masterpieces of comic observation, *Monsieur Hulot's Holiday* (1952) and *Mon Oncle* (1958), which satirize society's misguided preoccupation with gadgets. Albert Lamorisse's enchanting *Le Ballon Rouge* (1956), played by his small son and a balloon, had an equally universal appeal – 'no dialogue; no sentiment; tender, shy, exact as a pin prick, and beautiful'.

In 1956 young director Roger Vadim's first film *Et Dieu Créa la Femme* established a new sex symbol in Brigitte Bardot and La Nouvelle Vague in French cinema. This New Wave of directors played loosely and successfully with new techniques and new stars. Bardot's potent mixture of seething milky bosom and childish pout inspired a sea of sulky-mouthed and sloppy-haired imitators around the world. Jean-Paul Belmondo and Jean Seberg were the streetwise stars of Jean-Luc Godard's homage to the American gangster movie *A Bout de Souffle* (1959). Godard's audacious rejection of every convention of the narrative film made him the most innovative of all the Nouvelle Vague directors. Other outstanding ones were François Truffaut, *Les Quatre Cents Coups* (1959), Alain Resnais, *Hiroshima, Mon Amour* (1959), and Claude Chabrol, who also paid tribute to the American cinema, and particularly to Alfred Hitchcock, in his flamboyant and glossily decadent *Les Cousins* (1959).

Japanese and Indian cinema first achieved international recognition in the Fifties, when Akira Kurosawa's historical drama *Rashomon* (1951) and Satyajit Ray's anecdotal *Pather Panchali* (1954) won the Grands Prix at the Venice and Cannes Festivals respectively. Ray's film was the first of a trilogy which told the story of

*Opposite page*, Jean Gabin 'acts with increasing savour a French man of the people, brusquely talking without affectation in a deep, thistly voice'. In 1958 he played Simenon's inspector hero for the first time in *Maigret Tend un Piège*. 1952 PENN. *Above*, Rossano Brazzi, with 'a smile that's hardly there and a slippy but charming accent' achieved stardom playing Katharine Hepburn's irresistible Latin lover in David Lean's *Summer Madness*. 1955. PENN. *Top left*, Giulietta Masina and her husband Federico Fellini, 'great Italian artists whose medium is film'. 1958. WILLIAM KLEIN. *Far left*, Luchino Visconti, pioneer of Italian neo-realism, photographed by Irving Penn in 1955. *Left*, Silvana Mangano, the sultry heroine of the edible epic *Bitter Rice* (1948). 1954. PRIGENT.

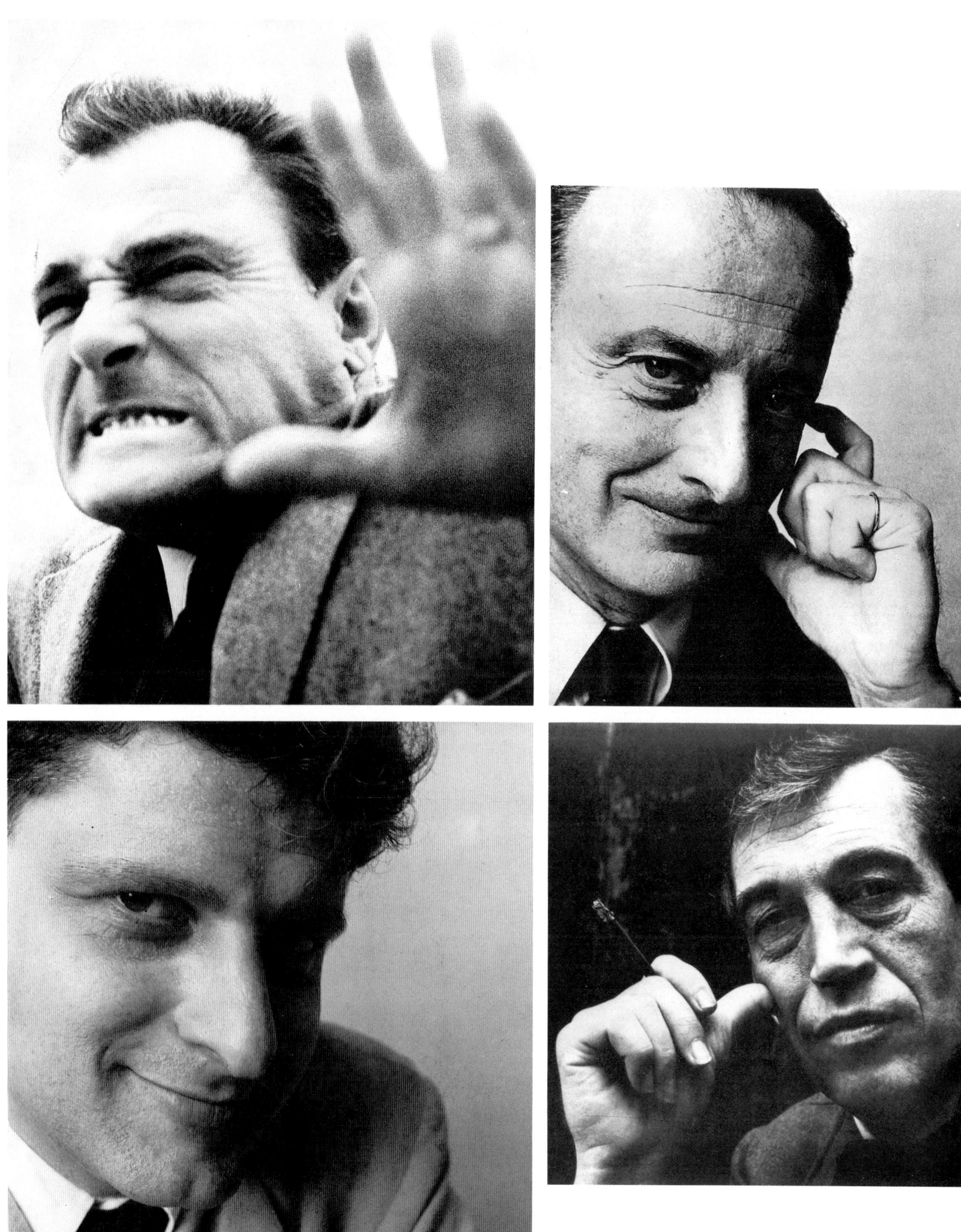

a poor Bengali family 'with a rapt fidelity that makes them masterpieces'.

The notorious Spanish director Luis Buñuel revived his international reputation with *Los Olvidados* (1950), an unsparing study of urchins brutalised by the slums of Mexico City. The Swedish Ingmar Bergman's anguished earnestness and bleak Nordic mood poetry made him the patron saint of the art houses, with films like *The Seventh Seal* (1956), *Wild Strawberries* (1957), and *The Face* (1958). But *Vogue* considered his metaphysical teasers 'an elaborate literary hoax full of veiled suggestions of doom that make Cocteau look explicit'.

In Italy the success of neo-realism produced a new generation of big international stars, including smouldering Latin bombshells Sophia Loren and Gina Lollobrigida. They starred in commercialized Italo-American comedies with token neo-realist settings as the excuse for a slice of risqué *dolce vita*. The earthy and magnificently endowed Silvana Mangano was the heroine of the edible epic *Bitter Rice* (1948). Luchino Visconti abandoned austerity for grand opera and richly decorative romantic costume pieces like *Senso* (1953) and *Le Notte Bianche* (1957).

Comedy was provided by Federico Fellini whose first major success was *La Strada* (1954). A carnival story photographed against desolate seascapes and sparse hills, with an obbligato of hurdy-gurdies and barkers, it starred his wife Giulietta Masina, playing 'with a funny, aching vulnerability that makes her Chaplin's heir'. Six years later Fellini's episodic exposé of Roman high society decadence, *La Dolce Vita* (1960), was an international *succes de scandale* which heralded a new golden age of Italian cinema.

**_Opposite top left,_ Mike Todd, the dynamic impresario husband of Elizabeth Taylor – 'The shriek photographed here was not rage, but fear when the wind caught the million-dollar glass door of his suite; the fear was not of breaking the door but of waking his wife'. 1957. ANTONY ARMSTRONG-JONES. _Bottom left,_ Paddy Chayefsky, author of _Marty, The Bachelor Party_ and _The Goddess._ 1958. PENN. _Top right,_ Fred Zinnemann, the Austrian-born director of _From Here to Eternity,_ 1953, which won eight Academy Awards. 1954. PENN. _Bottom right,_ John Huston, director of _The Asphalt Jungle_ and _The African Queen._ 1952. JOHN DEAKIN. _This page, right,_ the avant-garde Swedish director Ingmar Bergman. 1959. GEORG ODDNER.**

# VOGUE'S BOOK BAG

The fever of excitement generated by Sir Edmund Hillary's victory made his *The Ascent of Everest* the bestseller of 1953. 'This is the year of Everest,' announced *Vogue*, 'a year (like most years since the war) when books about the exploits of civilized explorers on wild-goose chases under very uncivilized conditions have once more made fiction look tame, homely and a bit dowdy. The more uninhibited our novelists become, the more the larger reading public seems to find relief and sense reality in a tidy tale of head-hunting according to the ancient rules prevailing along the Orinoco.

Thor Heyerdahl's Pacific odyssey *Kon-Tiki Expedition* (1950) and Jacques Cousteau's deep-sea diving saga *The Silent World* (1953) were outstanding among a glut of escapist bestsellers. The impact of William Golding's *Lord of the Flies* (1954), a shocking story of marooned English schoolboys slithering into dark barbarism, was equalled across the Atlantic by J.D. Salinger's *The Catcher in the Rye* (1951), a monologue by a 16-year-old boy whose bizarre adventures resembled an analyst's case history.

'I was there' war accounts came pouring off the printing presses – the memoirs of Field-Marshals Montgomery and Alanbrooke, Nicholas Monsarrat's *The Cruel Sea* (1951) and Peter Fleming's *Invasion 1940* (1957). James Jones' bitter and successful attack on the American military system, *From Here to Eternity* (1951), and Herman Wouk's *The Caine Mutiny* (1953) were phenomenally successful.

Sex entered the bestseller lists with Alfred Kinsey's report on *Sexual Behaviour in the Human Female* (1953) and a spate of salacious novels which were the subjects of notorious but unsuccessful obscenity trials. Most celebrated was Vladimir Nabokov's *Lolita* (1955); the story of a 40-year-old man's love affair with a twelve-year-

***Left***, **Françoise Sagan, 'a thin flash of success' with her first novel, *Bonjour Tristesse* (1954). 1959. PENN. *Opposite top left,* Jean Giono, 'like Colette, his predecessor in the Académie Goncourt, is a writer intoxicated by sensory perceptions'. 1955. BLUMENFELD. *Right,* Carson McCullers, young American author 'extraordinary, precocious maturity': she wrote the award-winning play *The Member of the Wedding* in 1950. 1951. PENN. *Opposite below,* Graham Greene, author of *The End of the Affair*, photographed by Irving Penn in 1951.**

old girl, it added a new word, 'nymphet', to the language. Another Russian, Boris Pasternak, took the world by storm with his searing historical epic *Dr Zhivago* (1958). 'It is like an enormous landscape with people "whose lives run parallel and close together but move at different speeds," until all are swept from the Russian Enlightenment to the Russian Revolution', wrote *Vogue*.

In England the established masters remained popular. In *The Ordeal of Gilbert Pinfold* (1957), 'bright young thing' of the Twenties Evelyn Waugh laid claim to 'voices, self-knowledge and other grown-up things' and Ivy Compton-Burnett continued her brilliantly malicious investigations of family life in *The Present and The Past* (1953). Graham Greene revealed a taste for espionage in *Our Man in Havana* (1958) and James Bond made his debut in Ian Fleming's *Casino Royale* (1953). Other important newcomers included Doris Lessing, who wrote 'with more foot-pounds than any other woman in this country', and the donnish Iris Murdoch. In his first novel, *Hemlock and After* (1952), Angus Wilson revealed himself as 'a furious satirist, with the energy and confidence of a pamphleteer'. C.P. Snow continued his analysis of Academia and Bureaucracy, *Strangers and Brothers*; Lawrence Durrell wrote his *Alexandria Quartet* (1957–60) and in 1951 Anthony Powell began his saga *A Dance to The Music of Time*.

But the most striking literary development of the decade was the arrival of the Angry Young Men with *Lucky Jim* (1954), the first novel by a young don at Swansea called Kingsley Amis. He was one of a new group of proudly provincial novelists, mostly grammar-school and red-brick university educated, who rejected 'high-brow' and 'phoney' attitudes and injected a new vitality into British fiction. John Braine's *Room at the Top* (1957), Alan Sillitoe's *Saturday Night and Sunday Morning* (1958), and Keith Waterhouse's *Billy Liar* (1959) dealt with working-class life from a working-class point of view and achieved notoriety overnight. The controversy over the 'U and Non-U' syndrome – the distinctions between upper and non-upper class speech – brought class conflicts to a new height of absurdity. The confidently 'U' Nancy Mitford, of 'Hons and Rebels' fame, gleefully spelt out the details in *Encounter* magazine and in an anthology called *Noblesse Oblige* (1956). She

helpfully pointed out 'that it is solely by their language that the upper classes nowadays are distinguished (since they are neither cleaner, richer, nor better educated than anybody else)' and all over England and America social reputations now depended upon not calling a napkin a 'serviette', or a pudding a 'sweet'. John Betjeman concluded *Noblesse Oblige* with a satirical poem, 'How To Get On In Society':

*Phone for the fish-knives, Norman,*
*As cook is a little unnerved;*
*You kiddies have crumpled the serviettes*
*And I must have things daintly served . . .*

Nancy Mitford brought a witty, colloquial touch to her biographies of *Madame de Pompadour* (1954), an 'Hon' if ever there was one, and *Voltaire in Love* (1957), whom she caught 'before he lost his teeth and his temper'.

In France Existentialism's most celebrated couple were Jean-Paul Sartre and Simone de Beauvoir, who, after the success of *The Mandarins* (1957) – 'a major piece of human nature study' – found her *metier* in autobiography – *Mémoires d'une Jeune Fille Rangée* (1958). A new group of writers – led by Samuel Beckett, *Molloy* (1955), and Nathalie Sarraute, *Martereau* (1953) – developed an alternative to the traditional novel, the *nouveau roman*. Time and reality were ignored and direct communication between novelist and reader was taboo. Not surprisingly the public preferred the work of less experimental writers, who included Jean Giono, *Le Hussard sur le Toit* (1952), Marguerite Yourcenar, *Les Mémoires d'Hadrian* (1952) and Louise de Vilmorin, *Madame de* (1951).

In 1955, a storm of controversy broke out over the authenticity of eight-year-old Minou Drouet's 'slimsy but charming school-of-Rimbaud poems'. Eighteen-year-old Françoise Sagan achieved a more durable celebrity after the success of her 'coolly witty, thoroughly amoral' first novel *Bonjour Tristesse* (1954), although *Vogue* soon noted the 'difficulty of being *terrible* when one is no longer quite such an *enfant*'.

**THE BALLAD OF THE SAD CAFÉ**
**by Carson McCullers, 1951**
Miss McCullers' disturbing talent is still little known here, though her reputation in America is on a level with that of Capote and Tennessee Williams. Her brilliant stories have the effect of a delayed thunderstorm or an unpaid bill.

*Opposite above,* Louise de Vilmorin, 'a virtuoso who plays with words and ideas like Paganini played the violin – her instrument is the French language'. 1955. CECIL BEATON. *Below left,* Simone de Beauvoir: 'in her *Mémoires d'une Jeune Fille Rangée* she writes absorbingly about Sartre, the man who has deeply influenced her life'. 1957. PENN. *Below right,* Ivy Compton-Burnett, 'an author whose strongly individual quality has secured the admiration of a small but almost fanatical public'. 1951. CECIL BEATON. *Above,* Evelyn Waugh, 'man of letters, man of wrath', his new novel *Men at Arms,* photographed by Irving Penn in 1952.

### THE OLD MAN AND THE SEA
**by Ernest Hemingway, 1952**

This is the story of an old professional fisherman, down on his luck, and his solitary three-day battle far out at sea with a gigantic marlin, 'in all his greatness and his glory'. In this struggle both are destroyed: but both are victorious. The book is impossible to classify, impossible to relate to anything else, except some passages in Homer, or the finest work of Ernest Hemingway.

### EAST OF EDEN
**by John Steinbeck, 1952**

In his new novel Steinbeck writes of pioneers, whores, monsters, and rural philosophers. A mature, engrossing story set in California's Salinas Valley between the end of the Civil War and 1918, this is probably Steinbeck's most important book in the twelve years since *The Grapes of Wrath*. Reflected through the coarse, violent, but often tender passages, is the kernel of Steinbeck's preoccupation: 'In uncertainty I am certain that underneath their topmost layers of frailty men want to be good and want to be loved. Indeed, most of their vices are attempted short cuts to love.'

### THE GO-BETWEEN
**by L.P. Hartley, 1953**

The most enjoyable novel of the year is L.P. Hartley's mesmeric incantation, *The Go-Between*, a story that – like so many contemporary novels – goes back into the past and finds a child and a summer holiday.

### LUCKY JIM
**by Kingsley Amis, 1954**

A first novel by a poet of increasing reputation – which is violently funny, wry, slapstick comedy about provincial university life, slightly early Waugh-ish in feeling, and brilliantly good.

### A HISTORY OF THE ENGLISH-SPEAKING PEOPLES: THE BIRTH OF BRITAIN and THE NEW WORLD
**by Sir Winston Churchill, 1956**

This meeting of historian and history-maker in one man is the divine accident of our time. How remarkable that there should have been a period in his career when he could give himself time to turn his long sight back over our history and write half a million words about it; and how

remarkable that the great statesman should also be a great writer, with a style as orotund and grandly striking as Macaulay's, a wry wit half-hidden in the texture, and a Shakespearean delight in the beat of words.

**ANGLO-SAXON ATTITUDES**
**by Angus Wilson, 1956**
This is his biggest-scale book so far. One feels that he has set out consciously to cover a large canvas: each character on the enormous cast list lives obsessively on a small island outside hailing distance of any other, and might be happier in a short story. But all the same Mr Wilson is a very good writer indeed, highly intelligent, with a tart edge on his observation (a satirist's quality in which the twentieth century is poor).

**THE OUTSIDER**
**by Colin Wilson, 1956**
Godot's stimulating successor in debate – this twenty-four-year-old has genius, uncanalized; a poet who writes only a raw prose, an alchemist with no hand for gold.

**A LEGACY**
**by Sybille Bedford, 1956**
This a complex character-study of a German family of sixty years ago; the style is beautifully exact and dry, and the dialogue has a fencing thrust. Sometimes the quick shifts of foothold recall Evelyn Waugh.

**THE FOUNTAIN OVERFLOWS**
**by Rebecca West, 1957**
This study of an erratic, gifted, sharply articulate family is a major work, for its author knows the meaning of many sorts of treason: her energetic percipience teases out the quirk in man that lets us defraud ourselves.

**AT LADY MOLLY'S**
**by Anthony Powell, 1957**
This is the fourth book in the *Music of Time* series (which has a marvellous promise of going on and on): it is incomparably stylish, funny and discerning. Mr Powell is the most entertaining writer in English now that Mr Waugh has started talking to himself. He also has the greater gift of rendering the grotesque without scorn, and of double-stopping the notes of elegy and irony.

***Opposite top left,*** **Kingsley Amis, 'a gutsily funny novelist who can scent phoneyness a mile off'. 1955. JOHN DEAKIN. *Top right,* Cecil Day Lewis, 'Irish by birth, his poetry has reflected the essence of the English scene and personality'. He was elected Professor of Poetry at Oxford in 1951. PENN. *Opposite below,* Ernest Hemingway with Spencer Tracy, who played the role of Santiago in the film of Hemingway's novel, *The Old Man and the Sea.* 1953. LELAND HAYWARD. *Above,* Boris Pasternak, whose novel, *Dr Zhivago,* 'illuminates half a century of Russian affairs; it restores a forgotten voice to world literature; and it is written with the deep concern and the heart that are part of the Russian embrace of life'. 1959. CORNELL CAPA.**

**BITTER LEMONS**
**by Lawrence Durrell, 1957**
Mr Durrell is a poet and a philhellene with ichor in the veins: no one could write more movingly of Cyprus, our squandered friend. His book is lit with lyric pleasures and a tolerance miraculously retained. Its simple perception makes one weep.

**NOT WAVING BUT DROWNING**
**by Stevie Smith, 1957**
Stevie Smith's book of new poems is drenched all through with the strange quality of the title, a sort of beautiful despair expressed in a laconic, isolated, matter-of-fact voice. The poems are very uneven, but the best are wry, and affecting, with the cross-beat of chuckles and cries that is Miss Smith's unique and unseating style.

**LEFTOVER LIFE TO KILL**
**by Caitlin Thomas, 1957**
Echoes of Dylan come off every page, but for all the reminders in her style this is a fiercely independent book: a mad masterpiece in a Dostoievsky prison, thrashing with the superb, crazed courage of a cripple refusing false limbs.

**MEMORIES OF A CATHOLIC GIRLHOOD**
**by Mary McCarthy, 1958**
A lucid, elating exploration of the upper reaches of childhood with only Miss McCarthy's imagination for company. That one does not grow bored or maddened testifies to her style, her masculine sensibility, and her winning malice. She had an appalling childhood; on the other hand she must have been a discomfiting child.

# BALLET-HOO

'Why the Ballet-hoo?' the choreographer Agnes de Mille asked *Vogue*'s readers in 1956. 'To make up a dance I need a pot of tea, walking space, privacy and an idea,' explained the intense and inventive niece of movie-mogul Cecil, who had pushed musical shows in a new direction with her dances for *Oklahoma!*. In 1954 she designed a tender *pas de deux* for Parisienne Zizi Jeanmaire's musical comedy ballet *The Girl in Pink Tights* on Broadway. Zizi scored a hit singing in 'a mad, wild voice', with her eyes made-up 'like the leading of a stained-glass window', her skin flour-white and her lips maroon, but to *Vogue* 'the wonder of Jeanmaire lies in her legs'.

'The most dynamic contemporary ballet company is the New York City Ballet – Balanchine, the greatest living classic choreographer, has given a new pure magic to dance, has widened the scope of classic ballet technique including its vocabulary,' declared *Vogue* after Lincoln Kirstein and Georges Balanchine's newly formed company made a dramatic début at Covent Garden in 1950. Their most spectacular success was Balanchine's version of *Firebird* with the 'tense, beautiful' American Indian Maria Tallchief. With his uninhibited use of acrobatic adagio Balanchine changed the course of classic ballet. Before Balanchine, male dancers caught ballerinas in jumping lifts at the waist; after Balanchine, partners caught wherever they could find leverage – by the knees, the arms, the elbows. Balanchine created many roles for his wife, the brilliant and witty ballerina Tanaquil LeClercq, among them that of the young girl who waltzes so enchantingly to death in *La Valse*. In 1957 he produced an austere and controversial ballet to music by Stravinsky, *Agon*.

Balanchine's younger associate was the dancer Jerome Robbins whose choreography often had 'the bubble of soda water'. *The Cage*, 'an extraordinarily explicit allegory about Men and Women, faintly disguised as the sex habit of the praying mantis', caused a stir danced with frightening intensity by Nora Kaye in 1951. Robbins turned his caustic humour into satiric movement in *The Pied Piper*, a carefree and exhilarating ballet with a marvellous use of rhythm. He recreated Nijinsky's scandalous *l'Après-midi d'un Faune* (1953) as a sensuous *pas de deux* encounter between two dancers in a rehearsal studio, dancing for their own pleasure before a mirror. In 1958 he formed Ballets USA

*Opposite,* Maria Tallchief, star of the New York City Ballet, dancing in Balanchine's *Firebird.* 1950. JOFFÉ. Norman Parkinson's record of the Bolshoi Ballet's London performance of *The Fountain of Bakhchisarai. Above,* the dance of the Tartar warriors in the last act displayed the marvellous powers of the Bolshoi's male dancers.

to take part in Gian-Carlo Menotti's festival at Spoleto. The company's success rested on the unusual degree of co-ordination between its dancers, which was strikingly displayed in *Moves,* a ballet without music, which Paris was the first to see in 1959. Another new company was that of Robert Joffrey, who assimilated and recreated in his eclectic ballets the most contemporary phenomena, like rock and roll and multimedia experiments.

In 1950 Richard Buckle counted 'four excellent Swan Queens' at Sadler's Wells. They included the red-headed beauty Moira Shearer, who 'surprises by her flashing radiance', and Margot Fonteyn, 'as perfect in classicism as the Parthenon'. Fonteyn created many rôles in the ballets of Frederick Ashton, most notably that of the doomed water-nymph in *Ondine* (1958) – Ashton's superlative statement about her gifts, with a score by Hans Werner Henze. In 1956 Sadler's Wells became the Royal Ballet and Fonteyn was created a Dame of the British Empire. *Vogue* dubbed her 'the *prima ballerina assoluta* of British ballet – a warm, lyrical artist who takes dance to its furthest remove from acrobatics'.

Another celebrated ballerina, Alicia Markova, founded the Festival Ballet company with Anton Dolin in 1950. They toured widely and gave seasons in London at the Festival Hall, attracting a very large public. After Markova left the company John Gilpin became its leading star, enjoying a greater popularity than any of its ballerinas.

As well as creating new ballets Frederick Ashton contributed to the popularity of revivals of nineteenth-century classics with a new version of *The Sleeping Beauty*, which was staged in a setting by Oliver Messel for Covent Garden's re-opening in 1946, and of Prokofiev's *Romeo and Juliet* (1955). He also created *Les Illuminations*, to an existing score by Benjamin Britten, for the New York City Ballet's sensational debut at Covent Garden in 1950. This was based on poems by the nineteenth-century symbolist poet Rimbaud, who was played by the darkly handsome Mexican dancer Nicholas Magallanes. The ballet's stylized sets were designed by Cecil Beaton, who wrote about their creation in *Vogue*.

The young South African choreographer John Cranko produced a comic masterpiece inspired by Gilbert and Sullivan, *Pineapple Poll* (1951), for the Sadler's Wells Theatre, before working at

***Opposite,* Alexander Lapauri and Maria Kondratiera in the Bolshoi Ballet's *The Fountain of Bakhchisarai.* *Above,* Dame Ninette de Valois, the vibrant martinet who in 1937 founded the Sadler's Wells Ballet Company, which became the Royal Ballet in 1956. 1955. *Top left,* the ethereal Alicia Markova. 1951. CECIL BEATON. *Top,* Margot Fonteyn. 1959. NORMAN PARKINSON. *Left,* Jerome Robbins, dynamic young choreographer with the New York City Ballet and of *West Side Story.* 1958. PENN.**

***Above,*** **Tanaquil LeClercq dancing Balanchine's *La Valse.* 1951. GJON MILI. *Opposite below left,* Balanchine and his wife, Maria Tallchief, photographed by Irving Penn in 1950. *Below right,* Zizi Jeanmaire, a 'ravishing delight' in her musical comedy ballet extravaganza *The Girl in Pink Tights.* 1954. RODERICK MACARTHUR. *Opposite above,* Carzou's spikily romantic set design for Act I of the Paris Opéra's production of *Giselle.* 1954.**

Covent Garden. There he staged a full-length ballet for which Britten wrote his only commissioned ballet score and John Piper designed the sets: *The Prince of the Pagodas* (1956) – 'a fairy tale full of the brilliant visual punning that is Cranko's idiom.' The exquisite Svetlana Beriosova danced the Princess and was tipped as Fonteyn's 'obvious successor'. In 1955 the spikily witty inventions of the young dancer Kenneth Macmillan's first ballet, *Danses Concertantes*, revealed an extraordinary and excitingly new choreographic talent.

At the Paris Opéra Jean Cocteau created a superb tragic role for Tamara Toumanova in *Phèdre* (1950), with a strong score by Auric. Serge Lifar, another of Diaghilev's protégés and the Opéra's *maître de ballet*, was still a performer of magnetic presence. He danced Albrecht in *Giselle* with the two great ballerinas Yvette Chauviré and Nina Vyroubova. Shortly before his departure from the Opéra in 1958 Lifar produced one of his most inspired creations, *Les Noces Fantastiques*, with music by Delannoy. Its poetic Celtic plot was conveyed with gripping intensity by Vyroubova and Peter van Dijk. Roland Petit gave a memorable performance as the hunted man-wolf in his own company's creation, *Le Loup* (1953), with Violette Verdy as the girl who loves him. But it was the sets and costumes by Carzou which caused a sensation with their brilliant colouring and delicate draughtsmanship.

'There is a blue moon over Covent Garden: the Bolshoi Company, never before seen in this country, opens its season on October 3rd and Ulanova the legend is here,' announced *Vogue* in 1956. The ballet in which she and the company dazzled Europe, Lavrovsky's *Romeo and Juliet*, had the sweeping grandeur of effect and heroic style of performance which was the very stuff of theatre. The men's 'virility, their wild and whirling speed, the ferocity of their attack' and the prodigious technique which took them across the stage in four standing leaps were a particular revelation. *Vogue* asked Norman Parkinson to photograph them performing and reflected: 'Nothing can tarnish the memory of a company who gave ballet their full selves; of the conductor who wept at the first-night applause and hugged David Webster like a child; of Ulanova, a white flame who made one forget to watch technique.'

# MUSIC NOTES

'The extraordinary phenomenon of the post-war European festival is a delight or a disease, according to how you look at it. Every year their number increases until now when every tiny village seems to be culturally *en fête*,' declared *Vogue* in 1954. In England Aldeburgh was 'the Bayreuth of Britten, its founder spirit and leading light' who dominated the English musical scene as composer, solo pianist, and conductor. Glyndebourne's father-figure was the prankish disciplinarian John Christie, a perfectionist who 'lags marvellously behind the age in his conception of patronage'. Christie's anachronism was not shared by the composer Gian-Carlo Menotti, who added The Festival of Two Worlds at Spoleto to the cultural merry-go-round in 1958. Its aim was to link Europe and America culturally – 'the Festival projects Menotti's passionate internationalism and commitment to the present,' enthused *Vogue*. 'Restless, flamboyant, a born coat-trailer for whom the bizarre has a chill and steady fascination', Menotti introduced the 21-year-old American conductor Thomas Schippers and gave director Luchino Visconti *carte blanche* to update Verdi's *Macbeth* to his favourite Romantic period.

The Festivals attracted the world's finest instrumentalists who included violinists Isaac Stern and Nathan Milstein, cellist Pierre Fournier, and pianists Artur Rubinstein, Clara Haskil and child prodigy Daniel Baremboim. The veteran cellist Pablo Casals and the violinist Georges Enesco ranked as 'the two greatest living interpretors of Bach'.

In 1950 John Amis reported on the British opera boom. Britten was embarking on *Billy Budd*, 'though all the sopranos and altos are threatening rebellion, as E.M. Forster's libretto is entirely male'; Michael Tippett, 'the greatest of the young', was working on his *Midsummer Marriage*, William Walton on *Troilus and Cressida*, and *The Pilgrim's Progress* by the grand old man of English music, Ralph Vaughan Williams, was soon to be presented at Covent Garden. Opera's popularity was aided and abetted by Britten's success and the influence of Lord Harewood, founder of *Opera* magazine, President of the English Opera Group and a director of the Royal Opera House. *Vogue* suggested his musical scholarship derived from reading the complete *Grove*, sent to him by the Princess Royal when a prisoner-of-war.

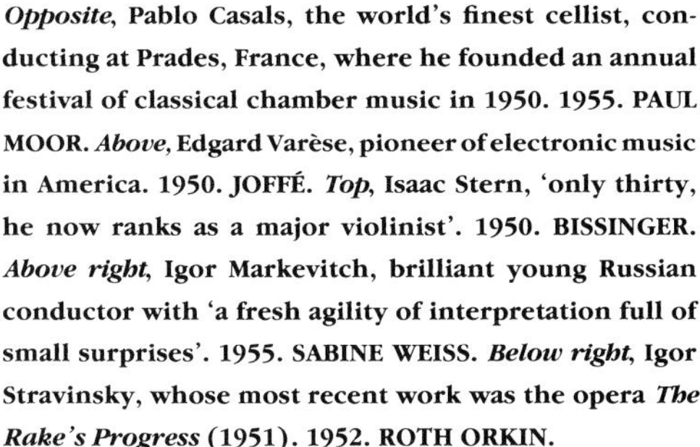

***Opposite,*** **Pablo Casals, the world's finest cellist, conducting at Prades, France, where he founded an annual festival of classical chamber music in 1950. 1955. PAUL MOOR. *Above,* Edgard Varèse, pioneer of electronic music in America. 1950. JOFFÉ. *Top,* Isaac Stern, 'only thirty, he now ranks as a major violinist'. 1950. BISSINGER. *Above right,* Igor Markevitch, brilliant young Russian conductor with 'a fresh agility of interpretation full of small surprises'. 1955. SABINE WEISS. *Below right,* Igor Stravinsky, whose most recent work was the opera *The Rake's Progress* (1951). 1952. ROTH ORKIN.**

In America Rudolf Bing revitalized the Metropolitan Opera by introducing such diversified talents as the choreographer Georges Balanchine, movie director Joseph Mankiewicz, and actor Alfred Lunt as opera-directors. Not all their productions were successful, but 'the results outweigh the complaints' reported *Vogue*.

Gian-Carlo Menotti triumphantly disproved all theories about contemporary problems being unsuitable for opera with *The Consul* (1950), a musical drama on a subject of terrible immediacy – the displaced person at the mercy of bureaucracy's brutality. 'A passionate *tour de force*,' exclaimed *Vogue*, 'it is a cry against the ignoble but safe sin of indifference to contemporary tragedy.' Menotti's brilliant young discovery, Patricia Neway, was a revelation as the tragic heroine. Menotti's next ventures were the television opera *Amahl and the Night Visitors* (1951) and *The Saint of Blecker Street* (1954), a melodrama of New York's Italian quarter. *Vogue* dubbed him 'an American phenomenon ... the only contemporary composer whose operas are almost always in performance somewhere and enjoyed by millions of TV watchers who would never go to an opera house.'

But the most important disseminator of contemporary and classical music to an even wider audience was the long-playing record, which made its appearance early in the decade. By its close there were thirty-one versions of Beethoven's *Fifth Symphony* available and Britons were buying 15 million classical records a year. Far from emptying the concert halls and opera houses, it filled them with a new, appreciative public. Leonard Bernstein, the composer of *West Side Story*, brought some showbusiness razzmatazz to the serious business of conducting the New York Philharmonic. At his

***Left*, Leonard Bernstein, composer of *West Side Story* and conductor of the New York Philharmonic. 1959. SABINE WEISS. *Opposite top left*, Benjamin Britten, composer of the operas *Billy Budd* (1951) and, for the Coronation, *Gloriana*. 1953. WICKHAM. *Opposite below*, Gian-Carlo Menotti, the Italian-born composer, librettist, and director of *The Consul* (1950), who founded the Spoleto Festival in 1958. 1950. HALLEY ERSKINE. *Opposite right*, the baroquely elegant Austrian conductor Herbert von Karajan, 'at forty-seven he is considered one of the great conductors of Europe'. 1955. PENN.**

'Preview' concerts at Carnegie Hall he ad-libbed to the audience, switched the programme around and generally gave things the improvisational quality of jazz, 'leading people to listen to works that would empty the Festival Hall'.

'Owing to the omnipresence of music in this age,' wrote John Amis in 1950, 'composers can be familiar with and write in any style they like – the result is that anything goes'. 'It seems hardly credible that Igor Stravinsky's next birthday will be his seventy-fifth,' mused *Vogue* six years later. 'In his compositions there has been no maturing in the sense of ageing: the new *Canticum Sacrum* is every bit as eager in experiment as *The Rite of Spring*, and far more testing of the listener.' But a new generation of composers was reacting against Stravinsky's neo-classicism and Schoenberg's atonalism. 'They want to change the whole sound and substance of the musical language and find new structural principles to govern their new materials. They regard the rhythmic aspect of music as the basis of structure and form and they recognize the affinity this concept brings between their own and Eastern musical systems, which are more like our jazz formulas, where a type of beat is the designing element, rather than a sonata form, a fugue, or some other convention as in our concert music.'

In America Edgard Varese pioneered electronic music and John Cage invented 'chance' music, which left the performer free to do as he wished within an established framework. In France Pierre Boulez extended the technique of serial organization to encompass a 'totally organized' whole, involving rhythm, tone, colour and dynamics – as in *Le Martineau sans Maître* (1954). Karlheinz Stockhausen became closely associated with the new sound world of tape and electronic music at the West German Radio Studio in Cologne. *Vogue* bemoaned British composers' avoidance of extremes – 'Britten, the most successful of our younger composers, leads the golden mean movement. His music is personal, but is daring only in its extraordinary use of the ordinary.'

The highest-paid prima donna in the world was the tempestuous Greek coloratura Maria Callas who made a dazzling London début, 'as thrilling as the sound of trumpets', in *Norma* at Covent Garden in 1953. A great actress and musician of astonishing versatility, she

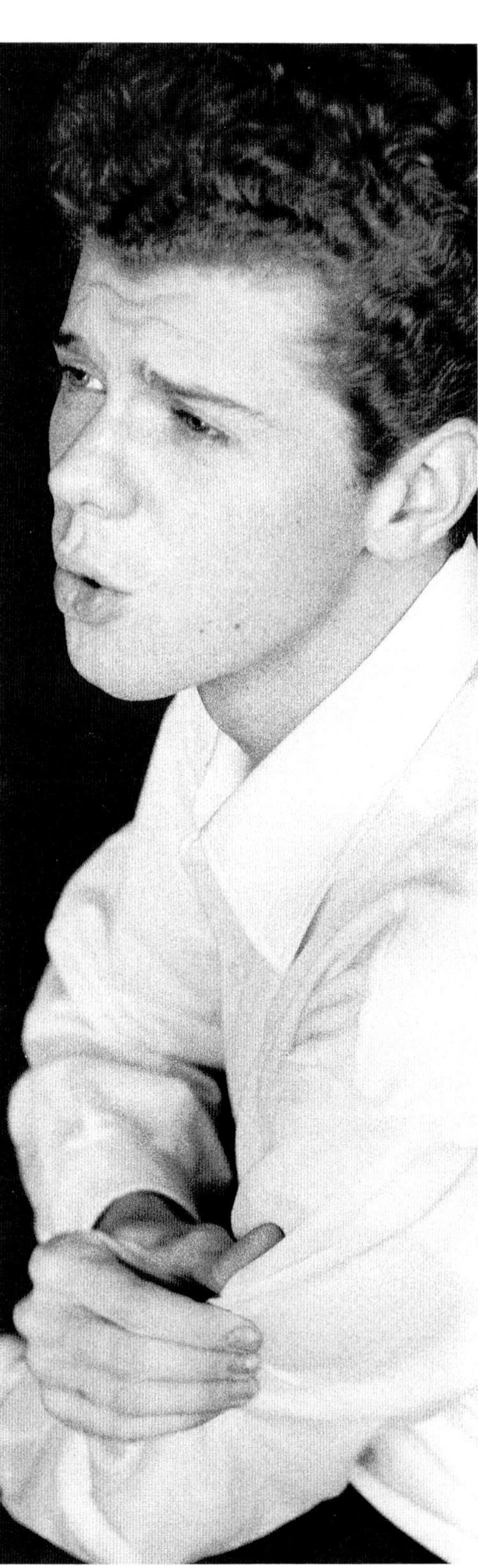

***Above***, **the Rumanian pianist Clara Haskil, 'her playing has a limpidity and an insight that give it a quality of clairvoyance'. 1956. SABINE WEISS. *Top*, Glenn Gould, 23-year-old Canadian pianist – 'tense, emaciated, Gould approaches his piano as he might an unbroken horse, bringing forth a tone both strong and lyrical'. 1956. *Left*, Van Cliburn, the 24-year-old Texan romantic virtuoso pianist. 1959. NORMAN PARKINSON. *Opposite*, Wanda Landowska, greatest of exponents of the harpsichord, now an almost legendary figure of seventy-eight. 1955. LANDSHOFF.**

discomfited the sopranos' union by becoming ten inches thinner than the accepted mean, and 'removing the excuse that blubber around the vocal cords is the staff of life to a beautiful voice'. America's most notorious soprano was Margaret Truman, who without first-rate talent battered a career for herself, 'in spite of the luck of being the President's daughter and the country's amused refusal to take her seriously'.

The velvet-voiced German baritone Dietrich Fischer-Dieskau shared a preference for *Lieder* singing with the Spanish *diva* Victoria de los Angeles and with his compatriot Elisabeth Schwarzkopf. She formed a powerful triumvirate with her husband Walter Legge, who founded London's Philharmonia Orchestra, and the Austrian conductor Herbert von Karajan. 'Brilliant with the catalytic quality which makes an orchestra play its heart out', he divided his greatness between London's Philharmonia, Berlin's Philharmonic and La Scala in Milan. But even von Karajan could not match the emotional impact of 87-year-old maestro Arturo Toscanini's final concert in 1954. At the end of the *Meistersinger* overture he dropped his baton on the floor and walked off to his dressing room, 'there to weep. He never returned to see the audience at Carnegie Hall stand applauding until someone turned on the house lights.'

**_Above_, Elizabeth Schwarzkopf, 'whose effortless soprano has made her the musical delight of Europe. . . . Her aim as a singer is to "communicate what is written" '. 1954. SABINE WEISS. _Below left_, Sena Jurinac, the vivid Bosnian soprano. 1958. _Below centre_, Victoria de los Angeles, golden-voiced Spanish soprano with a mezzo range, 'has sung with triumph at La Scala and at Covent Garden'. 1953. JOHN DEAKIN. _Below right_, Kathleen Ferrier, the radiant but tragically short-lived English contralto who died in 1953. 1952. NORMAN PARKINSON. _Opposite_, Maria Callas, 'the tempestuous idol: vulpine, divinely gifted, one of the rare singers who can act. She creates wherever she goes the climate of the prima donna: challenge, drama, music, temper – and love.' 1959. DOMINIC.**

# Design for Living

Like abstract painting, Fifties architecture exhibited a parallel concern with scale and rigorous simplification of forms – indeed with forms and textures and materials for their own sake. Le Corbusier, the presiding genius of the Modern Movement, conceived his architecture in ferro-concrete on a massive scale. His Unité d'habitation at Marseilles was designed as a machine for a community of 1600 to live in – not a block of flats but a small suburb. He revealed the 'true nature' of poured concrete by leaving the surface texture rough – a Brutalist dogma of truth to materials which was immensely influential. In imitation of Le Corbusier's credo of monumental austerity a multitude of dull, slab-like, flat-topped and straight-edged tower blocks rose rapidly along the skyline of almost every major city. Two significant examples were the United Nations building in New York (1950), and the Shell building in London (1958).

Lever House (1952) by Gordon Bunshaft, and the Seagram building (1955) by Mies van der Rohe and his pupil Philip Johnson, were both smooth and dazzling glazed towers. Standing almost opposite each other in New York, the Seagram Building rose in narrow bands of copper-tinted glass, but it was the plainer Lever House that was imitated all over America. Bunshaft, Johnson and Eero Saarinen, designer of the General Motors Technical Centre in Detroit, were dubbed 'Miesians' for their adherence to van der Rohe's famous dictum 'form follows function'. Van der Rohe's Lake Shore Drive apartment houses in Chicago and Farnsworth House, also in Illinois, were pure glass and steel boxes of classically symmetrical proportions. Vigorous black steel beams and contrasting mullions, precise in articulation and detail, became rhythmically ordered lines with voids of glass or brick between them.

The abstract forms of sculptors like Jean Arp and the random graffiti of abstract expressionist artists like Jackson Pollock were quickly absorbed into the decorative arts. The fashionable abstract free form was often counterbalanced by thin lines, as in the 'molecular-structure' motifs which reflected the era's optimistic preoccupation with scientific progress. Molecular structures and the thin, scratchy line used independently became the basis for patterns in every medium. In furniture design two important examples of the thin line were Ernest Race's 'Antelope' chair, designed for the Festival, and the American Harry Bertoia's 'Chicken-wire' chair, designed for Knoll International.

**_Far left_, Mies van der Rohe, 'a great moral force in architecture', and _left_, Philip Johnson, with a model of the Seagram building, which they designed in 1955. PENN.**

In America the look of furniture was transformed as the result of technical experimentation in the Forties. Under the patronage of the Museum of Modern Art there emerged a new school of designers of whom the most important was Charles Eames, who created an exciting organic international style. Eames' celebrated rosewood and hide lounge chair and ottoman of 1956 was a distillation of his ideals, which *Vogue* dubbed 'the most comfortable chair in the world'. With their moulded plastic and plywood chairs, Eames and his fellow architect/designer Eero Saarinen revolutionized seating design.

Organic forms were also found in the ubiquitous carved wood and glass tables, originally conceived in the Forties by the sculptor Isamu Noguchi; in the asymmetrical vases blown at Murano or at Scandinavian glassworks like Kosta; in the elegant silver of Georg Jensen; and in textile design. In architecture the style found a perfect expression in Frank Lloyd Wright's breathtaking spiral Guggenheim Museum in New York, completed in 1959.

With the light and open design of his own home Eames became one of the creators of the California Modern style interior, of which the most characteristic feature was the fluid interplay between indoor and outdoor space. 'Eames' house and its studio next door are like two great, bright, cube toys at first sight,' reported *Vogue*, 'inside, everyone responds to the free light-hearted space, the delightfully useless objects, arranged into simple patterns that never remain constant.' Matisse-inspired brightly coloured *découpage* patterns and Japanese-inspired open-plan handling of space were dominant influences in modern homes. *Vogue* featured the New York townhouse of the architect Edward Stone, its all-glass façade veiled with terrazzo lattice, and the 'floating' apartment of the industrial designer Raymond Loewy, which emulated the Japanese use of space and proportion 'to give an effect of serenity, and of limitless space'.

In Italy, the Milan Triennale exhibitions consistently presented innovative designs – 'combining a crisply modern approach with the warmth and richness of Italy's past'. *Vogue* dubbed Gio Ponti a 'universal man ... he has designed everything from chessmen to powerhouses'. He also edited the influential magazine *Domus*, a showcase of Italian design. While Ponti was a purist with restrained neo-classical taste some of his contemporaries like the furniture designer Carlo Mollino and the artist Piero Fornasetti adopted an imaginative, surreal style.

By contrast the warmly liveable Scandinavian Modern style embodied a respect for tradition, for craft, and for wood, and exercised a strong international influence. Typical Danish innovations were teakwood and matte finishes. In Britain a reaction to the austerity of Utility furniture was a popular outburst of 'Festival style' – clashing bright colours and changes of textures from brick and timber to stucco and glass, jazzy thin-line patterned wallpapers and carpets, and moulded and laminated 'contemporary' furniture with spindly legs entered millions of homes. But the Council of Industrial Design's evangelical zeal to promote good design encouraged a new generation of art college-trained designers such as David Mellor, Robert Heritage, and Terence Conran, who evolved a distinctive, realistic British Modern style.

Across the Atlantic the Modernist taste for functionality and simply ornamented forms was ignored by the designers at General Motors, Chrysler and Ford. Their streamlined automobiles, with exaggerated chrome trims, elaborate fins and fenders, were colourful and eye-catching symbols of consumerism. While these fuel-guzzling creations grew even bigger and more bizarre in design, in Europe the need for economy, the increasingly high price of fuel, and congested traffic conditions gave impetus to the development of simply styled, lighter and smaller cars with relatively inexpensive running costs. The three-wheeled Italian 'Isetta' bubble car was an extreme example. But it was British Leyland's revolutionary Mini Minor, designed by Alec Issigonis in 1959, which set a new European standard for small cars.

More dramatic than any developments in ground transport was the inaugural flight of BOAC's Comet airliner in 1952 – it heralded the world's first jetliner service and the advent of a new era in international travel.

**Above, l'Unité d'Habitation, Le Corbusier's vertical city at Marseilles. 1952. ROBERT DOISNEAU. *Below,* the curved aluminium and glass façade of Gio Ponti's 1951 Montecatini Company building in Milan. *Opposite, top left,* ceiling design with a flower image in reinforced concrete, by Nervi. 1954. Three New York landmarks: *Top right,* the terracotta lattice and glass façade of Edward Stone's townhouse. 1958. GUERRERO. *Bottom left,* Frank Lloyd Wright's luminous Guggenheim Museum, banded in light at night. 1959. EVELYN HOFER. *Bottom right,* Gordon Bunshaft's influential Lever house. 1952. KERTÈSZ.**

SOLOMON

*Above,* industrial designer Raymond Loewy's Japanese-inspired living room with *shoji* screened window, asymmetrically placed furniture (black bamboo armchairs designed by Loewy), on Matisse-reproduction rugs, and huge sea shells near a low Japanese table on the vinyl floor. 1955. RAWLINGS. *Above right,* Knoll Associates' idea for curtaining windows in a white room: vertical sliding panels of white fibreglass. 1951. KERTÈSZ. *Right,* Laverne Originals' new shape chair: a sling of black leather suspended from a three-legged frame of chromed steel. 1957. GRIGSBY.

*Above,* Le Corbusier, presiding genius of the Modern Movement. 1953. HERVÉ. ***Right,*** Le Corbusier's classic reclining chair in Chicago architect Benjamin Baldwin's living room. 1959. BALDWIN. ***Left,*** Gio Ponti's slender-limbed, black lacquer 'peasant' chair won the Museum of Modern Art's 1952 Good Design award. 1954. ***Below left,*** Ray and Charles Eames in their Californian living room. ***Below right,*** Piero Fornasetti's news-printed linen and china, with a centrepiece of newspaper roses. 1954.

# THE COMIC SPIRIT

'The public appetite for fun has never been more profoundly craving,' reported *Vogue* in 1952. Practically all of the comedians who satisfied this insatiable yearning appeared on television – even if their major roles lay in the movies, or radio, or nightclubs. In America the lovably dotty Lucille Ball's *I Love Lucy* show was the top rated programme for over five years. Other TV regulars were the short-sighted Phil Silvers, constantly evading regulations as Sergeant Bilko, and Gracie Allen, volubly silencing her perennial partner George Burns. 'After the ritual beginnings of gratitude and thank-you's, the present rhythm of most comic turns begins: the straight line, then the joke, the straight line, then the joke, until audiences, mesmerized by the moving ball of humour, laugh even when the rhythmic line breaks down.'

There was the same inevitability in Bob Hope's nagging insults about Bing Crosby's fortune, in the maddened slapstick of Jerry Lewis and Dean Martin. Groucho Marx was still the master of the apparently ad-lib insult and Bert Lahr's elegant, effortless mime and backswept speech, 'releasing syllables like pebbles from a reluctant rubber band', transcended burlesque.

England's best-loved new clown was the half-pint-sized Norman Wisdom. Nervous, dim-witted, but constantly resilient, he charmed the misfit in everyone with his battered face and sheer inability at everything. The star of many stage and TV shows, he soon became Rank's biggest money-earner in a series of screwball films. His principal rival was Ian Carmichael, who personified the English public school silly-ass. He successfully dithered from one dilemma to another in films like the Boulting brothers' satires on big business and scholarship, *I'm All Right Jack* (1959) and *Lucky Jim* (1957).

Funny ladies were also much in demand. The worldly-wise and Cockney-shrewd Dora Bryan was the darling dead-pan Dora of countless studies of bright barmaids and terrible tots, while Hermione Baddeley reminded *Vogue* of 'a unique cross between Cleopatra and the wife of Bath'. Hermione Gingold distilled cheerful poison as Drusilla Doom, the chic and sibilant vampire-lady of awful habits and viperish tongue in her weekly radio series. 'With one exclamation in her gruesome bass voice and one loathing stab of the finger, she can undermine every idea of innocence one ever had,' reported

*Vogue*. Joyce Grenfell was another elegant and murderous satirist. Her acute ear for parody was the basis of her highly successful one-woman show in London and on Broadway.

Radio comedy was also enlivened by the irreverent Goons – alias Peter Sellers, Harry Secombe and Spike Milligan. With surreal wit they used the freedom of radio to leap through time and space in pursuit of a purely verbal joke, developing humour into a non-figurative art. 'No build-up, and no hanging around for the unities to catch up; just a helplessly funny, cosmic disinhibitedness.' The ageless Crazy Gang carried on the tradition of the old music halls at the Victoria Palace theatre in an atmosphere of gleeful chaos and good clean dirty jokes 'so old and yet so vigorous that the public will keep flocking to see the Gang so long as they have strength left to knock over a ladder and squirt a syphon down each other's underwear'. Limitlessly vulgar and greedily anarchic they paddled about dressed as lady hikers or revolting Little Lord Fauntleroys in blue satin rompers.

'In the theatre the Englishman likes his comics to be traditionalist,' wrote Siriol Hugh Jones. 'He suspects the new joke, the novel approach, the unexpected twist to a situation. He knows that Gracie Fields will sing "Sally", and "I never laffed so mooch in all me life", if he shouts for them, and he's been shouting for years for her well-known Lancashire gags about reluctant bridegrooms and insistent brides. He knows and loves Leslie Henson's familiar gin-and-fog croak, intimate as a conman's first approach, and the endless series of tortured and ecstatic expressions that outrage his goldfish features. He knows George Formby's grin and his ukelele and his rude leer like the guffaw of a recalcitrant milkman's horse; he knows the awesome familiarity of Wilfred Pickles, to whom nothing is sacred and whose every nudge guarantees a guilty nationwide guffaw produced by "sharing" on a scale hitherto known only to Buchmanites; he knows Cecily Courtneidge's hearty thigh-slapping gusto; Eddie Gray's gloomy, fierce bursts of aggression; Fred Emney's vast curves and tiny hostile eye like a baby rogue elephant in a fit of the sulks. He knows and recognizes instantly the weaving, bobbing gestures, the dubious stare and the great Falstaffian cowardice of Sid Field, King of the Spivs.'

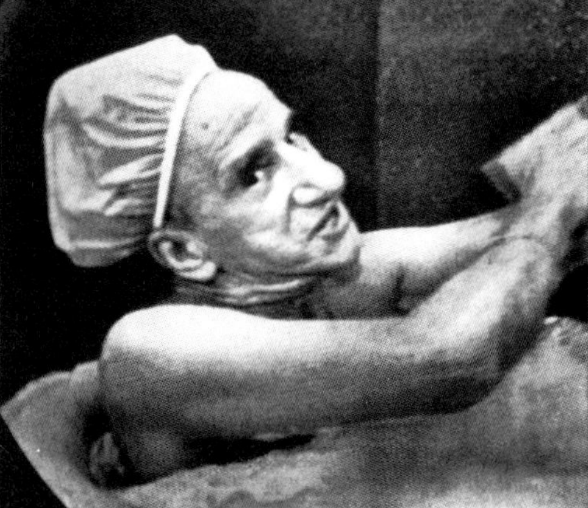

**Opposite**, **Phil Silvers, star of the new musical comedy, *Top Banana*, 1951. HALLEY ERSKINE. *Above*, Groucho Marx, 'most verbal of the Brothers, wise-cracking at moments of ghastly inopportunity'. 1958. PENN. *Top*, Sid Caesar, 'the humour of exaggerated pantomime, an extraordinary ear for double-talk in any language'. 1952. PENN. *Above right*, Jimmy Durante, 'the gravelled look of outrage and the sudden rippled laugh'. 1952. PENN. *Below right*, Jack Benny, 'as timed as a railroad man's watch'. 1952. PENN.**

***Opposite top left,*** 'this jaundiced patriot is one of the participants in the Goons' weird ***Running, Jumping and Standing Still Film,*** one of the treasures of the Edinburgh Festival'. 1959. ***Bottom left,*** Norman Wisdom, 'his fundamental appeal lies in copelessness: life overwhelms him'. 1954. JOHN DEAKIN. ***Opposite top right,*** Frankie Howerd photographed by Claude Virgin in 1957. ***Bottom right,*** Dora Bryan, 'the darling dead-pan-Dora of countless studies of bright barmaids and terrible tots'. 1953. JOHN DEAKIN. ***Above,*** Millicent Martin, 'cross-eyed and feather-brained', photographed by Norman Parkinson in 1959. ***Above right,*** Comic conjuror Tommy Cooper, 'his tricks never quite succeed, and his patter is a constant cover-up for terrible gaffes', with Arthur Askey. 1957. NORMAN PARKINSON. ***Right,*** Leslie Henson, 'the Englishman knows and loves his familiar gin-and-fog croak and the endless series of tortured and ecstatic expressions that outrage his goldfish features'. 1952. JOHN DEAKIN. ***Far right,*** Spike Milligan, centripetal Goon 'has given a new texture to humour: a clear, skid-surfaced, surreal wit'. 1957. ANTONY ARMSTRONG-JONES.

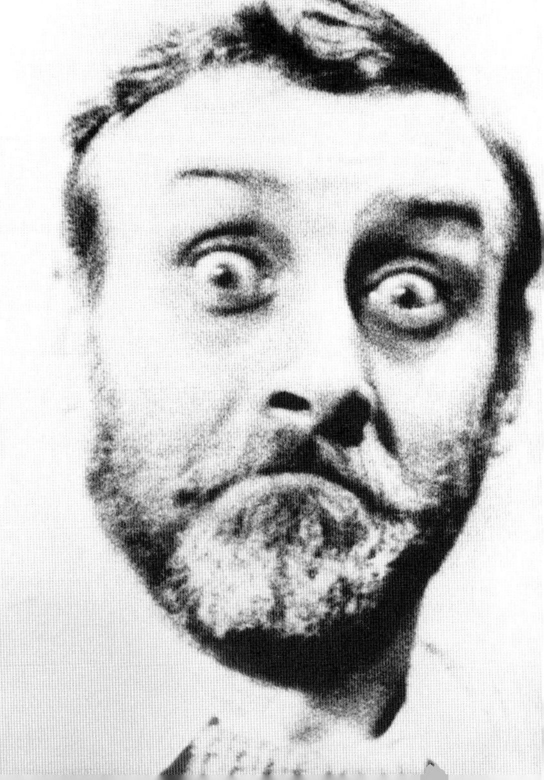

# THE GASTRONOMIC MAP

In the Fifties many of *Vogue*'s readers had to manage without servants and the 'Art of Entertaining' series tried to make life easier for people who had 'to housekeep without a cook'. American *Vogue* heralded the New Ice Age, praising the freezer as the most dependable source of nourishment the country had ever known and 'Connoisseur on Cannery Row' gave gourmet recipes for 'fine cooking out of a can'. In England Elizabeth David realized that rationing, which continued until 1954, and the disappearance of servants 'have led Englishwomen to take a far greater interest in food than was formerly considered polite' and her book *Mediterranean Food* (1950) created a culinary revolution. Her conviction that good cooking was honest, sincere and simple, and insistence on the best basic ingredients, were a vivid contrast to the synthetic ingredients of wartime and the elaborate technicolor creations of so-called 'haute cuisine'. She wrote in *Vogue*: 'Many sins have been committed in its name; and for financial and economic reasons it is becoming rare, even in France. The feeling of our time is for simpler food, simply presented; not that this is necessarily easier to achieve than haute cuisine; it demands less time and expense, but if anything a more genuine feeling for cookery and a truer taste.'

In 1956 Elizabeth David started writing a monthly series of articles on the finest food in season, followed by a series on French regional cooking and 'The Tools of the Trade'. She gave instructions on how to eat a globe artichoke, how to cook a perfect omelette and toss a perfect salad, and introduced such Mediterranean novelties as courgettes and aubergines, basil and tarragon, as well as classic dishes like quiche Lorraine, taramasalata and coq au vin.

In 1951 the first *Good Food Guide* was published and American *Vogue*'s guide to London restaurants reported, 'No matter what our relations in Chicago think, hunger-pinched Britons are not fainting in platoons in Trafalgar Square. Almost everything is available in good supply now, though napkins are still not as plentiful as they should be, and meat and eggs are still short.' They found that Britain's pubs, 'oases of cut glass and mahogany – offer some of the best food in the country', that 'one of London's nicest extravagances is the Oyster House', and that 'the four Corner Houses of the Lyons tea-

shop chain serve food of good quality at very reasonable prices'. For the Festival *Vogue*'s readers were advised to 'go frankly native' for their foreign visitors, 'giving only dishes that are typically British – we may not be able to provide sirloins of Scotch beef, or regale them with saddles of Welsh lamb, still there remains much that we can do on our slender ration, and the fish that swim about these shores are second to none'. The Coronation found *Vogue* preparing for another siege of overseas visitors to entertain with advice on 'How to cope with Coronation guests' and a feature on 'Coronation Cuisine – a preview of some of the dishes several well known restaurants will star in Coronation week'.

The hostess had become the International Hostess, from France, England, Italy and America, and each published her favourite recipes in *Vogue*. Young American editor Mrs William Rayner was dispatched to Paris in reply to an invitation from Maxim's Academy 'to acquire that special Parisian brio which is the crowning touch of the perfect hostess'. An offspring of the famous restaurant, Maxim's Academy was run by the Comtesse Guy de Toulouse-Lautrec who also contributed articles to *Vogue*. Her students explored the pleasures and pitfalls of *haute cuisine* and assimilated such helpful pointers as 'the guests can wait for a soufflé, a soufflé can't wait for the guests'.

'Eat your holiday souvenirs!' exclaimed food writer Robin McDougall: 'When you dine out and the soup, the fish, the meat and the salad are all heavily laced with garlic, you can be pretty sure your hosts are just back from Provence. If there is grated Parmesan with the soup and with the risotto, and the supreme of chicken is served under a cheese sauce, your hosts are just back from Italy. Not that everything is drenched with garlic in Provence or covered with cheese in Italy; it is just that your hosts' nostalgia has run away with them'. Creole and Indian, Spanish and Austrian cuisines all received their culinary due in *Vogue,* which also reported on 'London's pleasure in the book *Around the World in 80 Dishes*, in which Lesley Blanch ... tours the globe, putting each dish in its place with a sharp anecdote' and on Alice B. Toklas' 'rather weird yet wonderful kitchen compendium – filled with strange recipes like "Chicken in Half Mourning" and "Virgin Sauce".'

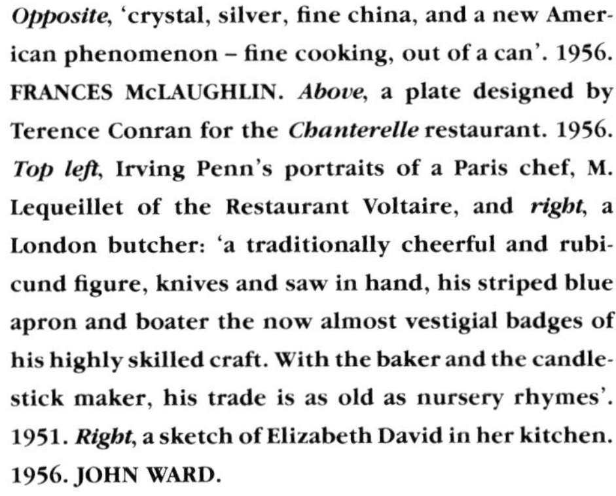
***Opposite,*** **'crystal, silver, fine china, and a new American phenomenon – fine cooking, out of a can'. 1956. FRANCES McLAUGHLIN. *Above,* a plate designed by Terence Conran for the *Chanterelle* restaurant. 1956. *Top left,* Irving Penn's portraits of a Paris chef, M. Lequeillet of the Restaurant Voltaire, and *right,* a London butcher: 'a traditionally cheerful and rubicund figure, knives and saw in hand, his striped blue apron and boater the now almost vestigial badges of his highly skilled craft. With the baker and the candlestick maker, his trade is as old as nursery rhymes'. 1951. *Right,* a sketch of Elizabeth David in her kitchen. 1956. JOHN WARD.**

The range of imported specialities grew ever wider and in 1957 it was possible to find 'a remarkable collection of wines and food, many of them new to this country – such delights as a special soy sauce from Hong Kong, Italian wafers from Montecatini, a liqueur from the Basque country, a French cheese now imported', and at the new Café Chambord Gourmet shop in New York 'such especially good frozen sauces as Périgordine with truffles and sauce Véronique'. Elizabeth David observed: 'So odd has the system of export and import become that the ingredients of many Mediterranean dishes are not only easier to come by in London than the materials of plain English cooking but sometimes more plentiful than they are abroad.'

*Vogue* was able to report encouragingly on the increasing number and type of good restaurants in London, announcing, 'It is time we began to be proud of the fact that we can eat cheaply in London better than anywhere else in the world, and that our expensive restaurants like the Mirabelle, the Caprice or La Réserve can produce a meal as fine as anything to be had in Paris.' Elizabeth David's influence was felt not only in kitchens throughout the country but in the gradual improvement of standards in restaurants, particularly in those of a completely new type which sprang up all over London: the cosy, intimate, 'neighbourhood' restaurant, the little place round the corner where the local inhabitants could get a good dinner without having to go as far as the West End. Two favourites were the Chanterelle in the Old Brompton Road, designed by Terence Conran, who also started a chain of Scandinavian-style soup kitchens, and La Popote in Walton Street, decorated by the theatre designer Loudon Sainthill. The multitude of less professional restaurants led *Vogue* to complain: 'Nowadays every other man writing a thesis or an obscene book decides to open a bistro with the other hand, equipped with a taste for garlic, a friend who's a dab at decorating, and a clutch of débutantes or medical students with the required attitude of happy fatality.'

Another development observed was the growing popularity of all things Oriental, including food. 'There have always been good Chinese and Indian restaurants in London and today they are flourishing as never before. London now boasts the only Siamese restaurant in Europe and the only Japanese restaurant in England – the most difficult thing to find in London is good English food.' The reaction to over-exoticism was 'the chic, which now seems absolute, of eating steak-and-kidney pudding at great expense in the restaurants where any unperverted person would have something more patrician and less like home . . .'.

A new addition to the gastronomic scene were the ubiquitous Italian coffee bars which multiplied throughout England on the strength of the Gaggia Espresso machine, and were decorated in every imaginable style from Regency to South Bank Modern. These were frequented by the new welfare state young, university and art students, practised at eking out a cup of espresso all day while writing theses and novels, before jiving or rock 'n' rolling all night at jazz clubs or dance halls. *Vogue* noted the 'crowded, slightly jazzy El Cubano in the Brompton Road' with tropical decor and West Indian waiters; Heaven and Hell, where 'Heaven is rosy and has cherubs; Hell, of Stygian darkness lit only by the red eyes of devils'; or for a change of milieu the studiously quiet Partisan on Charlotte Street, 'a haunt of left-wing intellectuals'.

New cocktails were constantly being shaken around the globe, including such classics as the Screwdriver and the Bloody Mary, the Margarita and the Piña Colada, the Kir and the Black Russian. Exoticism and fads in dining out continued to multiply with *Vogue* enthusing over such delights as freshly shelled sea urchins

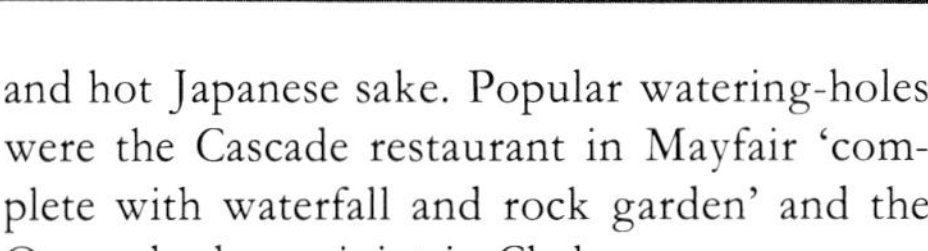

***Left***, **'Eric Portman and Margaret Leighton, the stars of Terence Rattigan's powerful Broadway hit, *Separate Tables*, here face a remarkable collection of wines and foods, many of them new to this country'. 1957. PENN. *Above*, the Comtesse de Toulouse-Lautrec of Maxim's Academy, warns her cooking class (who include Vogue's Mrs William Rayner): 'Fire is the enemy, watch the flame'. 1959. DOISNEAU. *Below*, the actress Ilka Chase, daughter of Vogue's legendary editor Edna Woolman Chase, and author of a 'Culinary guide for imbeciles who like to eat'. 1955. RAWLINGS.**

and hot Japanese sake. Popular watering-holes were the Cascade restaurant in Mayfair 'complete with waterfall and rock garden' and the Orrery barbecue joint in Chelsea.

In Paris there was the Acapulco, where Mexican food and serenading Mariachis were the attractions, and the Caviarteria, serving Beluga until 7am. The new smart gathering place for the young was the luminous drugstore, near the Étoile, which included among its specialities banana splits, theatre tickets, art books, ice cream sodas, whisky, a seafood bar for sea urchins, and a barbershop where notable figures such as Jean Pierre Aumont and Claude Dauphin had their hair cut.

America's latest restaurant attraction was the only private dining-room on a train – the Sante Fé's new Super Chief which ran between Los Angeles and Chicago. In New York the spectacular new Seagram building housed 'the compulsive, art-orientated cafeteria', The Brasserie, open for 24 hours a day and serving fromage-burgers on plates designed by Picasso. At The Four Seasons restaurant the paintings were by Jackson Pollock, Miró and Picasso.

Outside Rome's newest restaurant, Da Meo Patacca, a cowboy on horseback gave parking directions, and *Vogue* observed: 'The Italian influences are even filtering into Melbourne, Australia: the pizza places, the cafe espresso houses, the Roman restaurants with lovely, slippery food.'

# PICTURES OF CHRISTMAS

Another Christmas has come and gone. Aunt Ruth has once again been 'wonderful', but who wouldn't be on her income? Shy, dowdy Cousin May has been a creature transformed, with sparkling eye and almost a witty tongue, if, and people are strangely naïve, you like that sort of elfin charm; dear old Rodney, despite his age-old jokes and tedious reminiscences, has obviously enjoyed every moment of it, but then if one is completely insensitive...: but, for poor Hamish, and Stephanie, and Aunt Isobel, so much more intelligent and sensitive and sophisticated, Christmas has once again been hell. By their silences, their sudden sharp digs, their little, hysterical, sarcastic laughs, they make sure, at any rate, that no one who goes on the family Boxing Day walk can remain unaware of the strain the whole thing has meant for them; make doubly sure that the simple, the energetic and the unselfconscious, who have passed a happy Christmas, shall be made aware of the appalling failure the family reunion has really been.

What can they do about it, these more intelligent, more sensitive people, for whom the absurdity, the forced gaiety, the routine celebration, the bony bareness of the family skeleton stick out so sharply from behind the paper chains and the Christmas tree? It would be easier for them, perhaps, if the season retained some of its old, serious, religious aspect, but Christmas in England still remains predominantly the jolly, sentimental, eating and drinking, pagan family celebration that it has been for the last eighty years. Here and there, it is true, the fundamental Christian spirit has always survived – Jennifer and William still have to accompany Mother to Church; here and there, the Christian significance has lately resurrected itself among the younger generation – Father tries so hard to say the right thing when Humphrey and Ann return from early service; but, by and large, it is a curious, attenuated version of the late-Victorian family orgy which most of us attend.

It is, perhaps, this gradual shrinking of the feast that makes it most difficult for those who do not fit in. One could roister and brim over and keep the fun up and perform the other rather demanding activities that Family Christmas asks if there were only the food and drink on the great late-Victorian scale to sustain such high spirits; one could forget oneself in the general give and take, if families were more on the Victorian scale: after all, Aunt Estelle with the new treatment for her back, and Aunt Evelyn, brimming over with stories of her divorce, are obviously taking from the start, and, in a small family, it leaves so few to give.

Nevertheless, if Christmas is to be enjoyed, it is necessary to throw oneself into a rôle. For the selfconscious, perhaps, the safest rôle is the 'Great Understander'. Helping to bridge over the difficult moment is an easy and very rewarding rôle for the sophisticated who find Family Christmas 'difficult'. Who was the one who laughed at Aunt Nora's joke, when she went one too far, and yet somehow saw that she didn't tell another 'near the knuckle' story? Who was the one who smiled with Cyril, seventeen and highbrow, when he would introduce names like Sartre and Kierkegaard into the family paper games? Who listened to Cousin Monica on the Boxing Day walk, and agreed that if he didn't ring up on Thursday there was no earthly reason why she shouldn't ring, as long as she did it quite casually? Or to Uncle Arthur when he illustrated the retreat from the Marne with spoons and salt cellars? The great, the popular Understander, of course – she or he who had always before found Christmas such a 'difficult' time.

**Angus Wilson**

The Tree stood in the centre of the domed conservatory, dark, majestic, and indifferent, amid the pots of pink, and pale pink, and white cyclamen; boxes writhing with tinsel; bugles and wicked-coloured witch balls: with candles of honest colours like chalks – red, blue, green and orange. The stiff boughs began to droop beneath the glittering weight of their regalia; the tree shivered and the bugles made a faint silver trembling. The candles began to strike impertinent attitudes – somebody fetched a pair of steps. The fairy queen in white and gold, with odd-ended golden hair, because one of the children had cut it like his mamma, was lashed to the summit of the tree, where she might survey a

sea of presents – brown, and white, and holly-papered; long, and large, and round, and small. Objects whose identity could not be concealed – a tricycle with rubber handlebars like the whiskers of a commissionaire – were heaped with better kept secrets: hard little white boxes containing some precious piece of Sicilian jewellery for one of the three young women; flat square boxes (Irish handkerchiefs for a nanny); brown boxes with weapons or masks or fireworks for boys. Parcels of books: about gardening, about love, about murder, about moths, about desert islands, about eccentrics, about food, about fifty dull things to do on a rainy day. Painful parcels of railway track, and alarming parcels of stuffed animals moaning and gibbering in their wrappings. Boxes of shavings and glass; envelopes reeking of soft expensive leather.

At eleven the conservatory was locked, and the women went to collect the creaking distorted golf stockings for the children's dawn.

At half past five the first child woke. At twenty to six, blue with cold, it sat at the end of its bed, on a broken clockwork beetle, eating the wreck of a tangerine. Its bed was littered with paper and the only warm thing was some chocolate money under its pillow.

Christmas had begun. Not white, but pretty, the maids agreed, drinking boiling brown tea in their cardigans. The sky was dense and breathless, loaded with snow which had begun to drift down in large casual fragments when, hours later, they left the church. . . .

They all went to church, wearing their Christmas clothes: their fur hats, their Russian leather boots with countless buttons, their cloaks like highwaymen. They sang 'Emmanuel' and 'Oh come, all ye faithful' in the small church decorated with white and yellow chrysanthemums, and two rows of little steaming choirboys.

Then I watched them eat their turkey, plum pudding, crystallized fruits, almonds, raisins, mince-pies, oranges, Stilton cheese, walnuts, pineapples, preserved ginger and brandy, until the table was a vast litter of boxes of white lace paper, nutshells, spilled coffee, sugar and brown pudding sixpences.

Later, I saw the tree lit to a mountainous maze of candles through the grey of the conservatory glass.

**Elizabeth Jane Howard**

***Above,*** **the Banqueting Room of the Royal Pavilion, Brighton, brought to life and photographed by Anthony Denney. 1958.** ***Opposite,*** **'Two of the real Christmas experts – the children – have the wreath situation well in hand. They know how a tree should be trimmed; how a crêche should be arranged; and that the Christmas centrepiece is there to be eaten'. 1958. KATHRYN ABBE.**

# ADVERTISING IN VOGUE

As controls of foods, petrol and on hire purchase agreements in Britain were lifted in the early Fifties the country's new mood of economic prosperity stimulated sales and demand for all types of consumer goods. The tempo of marketing increased and new brands were introduced at an ever faster rate; for the first time since the war manufacturers found themselves in competition. Advertisers and agencies struggled to find some claim to uniqueness which would set their product apart from the rest. *Vogue*'s advertisers naturally appealed to the magazine's style-conscious readers. The Hillman Minx saloon car was 'top fashion around the world', 'Vogue' cigarettes were 'the fashion cigarette. In five glamorous pastel shades', and Canadian Pacific's 'Scenic Dome Streamliner' was 'a blueprint for fashion in trains'.

*Vogue*'s advertising pages were an integral part of the magazine, and in 1948 an annual advertising award was introduced for good design. As in *Vogue*'s editorial pages, photography was now used more than drawings, but illustrators like René Gruau created striking graphic images for prestigious Paris couture houses, such as Dior and Jean Cocteau and Salvador Dali lent artistic cachet to the cosmetic houses of Elizabeth Arden and Elgin American. Celebrities and film stars continued to endorse products – and even places: Noel Coward enticed tourists to Jamaica, Claudette Colbert enthused 'Avon lipsticks are sensational!', Jane Wyman, (the former Mrs Ronald Reagan), and Joan Crawford were the proud owners of Evans handbags, and Natalie Wood used Dorothy Perkins cosmetics 'to accent her natural loveliness'.

In the Fifties psychologists moved into the advertising world like witch doctors with a magic formula, convincing sales directors that you could make people believe anything you wanted if you probed the depths of the unconscious mind. One series of ads appealed to a subconscious streak of feminine exhibitionism: 'I dreamed I stopped the traffic in my Maiden-

***Above***, **'Never before has it been possible to see spectacular Canada from a Dome train! At last this thrill is yours aboard *The Canadian*! Now you can see 2,881 miles of scenic beauty on the longest Dome ride in the world!' Canadian Pacific. 1955. *Opposite*, Jamaican habitué Noel Coward doing his bit for tourism in 1958.**

# come to Jamaica—it's no place like home

Think of the most beautiful place you've yet seen in the world. Jamaica is more so, *outrageously* so. Jamaica's the place to get away *with* it and/or get away *from* it. An enthused international "Who's Who" flocks here to do as it pleases. The sun shines all the time. In Jamaica you can find perfect peace. Yet the island pulses with theatrical contrasts between new and old, civilized and primitive. If you hanker to see the world, better do that first. Because once here, Jamaica will bewitch you—and may become all of the world you'll ever care to see.

not a word

never at night

peace, peace, perfect peace... and one's loved ones far away

Jamaica, for me, is the loveliest island in the world

Noël Coward

come to Jamaica—it's not far from home

**JAMAICA IN THE WEST INDIES.** Jamaica Tourist Board • New York • Chicago • Miami • Toronto, Canada • Kingston, Jamaica, W. I. **SEE YOUR TRAVEL AGENT**

This is the day of history . . . the
day of which, through years ahead, men will thrill
with pride and say, 'I too was there' . . .
And the Drakes, the Raleighs, the
Shakespeares – indeed all who have added
lustre to Britain's name – maybe will smile
the smile of satisfaction and foreknowledge . . . for
another Elizabeth has come and all the world
has gained a Queen. So ring out bells!
Blow trumpets! Herald with your fanfare
the dawn of another Golden Age . . .
Coronation Day 1953
By Appointment
Biscuit Manufacturers
to the late King George VI.
McVitie & Price Ltd.
McVitie & Price Ltd.
MAKERS OF FINEST QUALITY BISCUITS
Edinburgh · London · Manchester

form bra'. Every type of product now sought to acquire a memorable 'brand image' – from Esso petrol's friendly tiger and the Marlboro cigarette cowboy to Chanel's instantly recognizable No 5 perfume bottle. Advertising campaigns became more elaborate than ever before: Stephen Potter of Schweppes introduced '*Schweppsylvania*', 49th of the United States', and '*Schweppshire*' in Britain, with a series of maps and guides drawn by Loudon Sainthill and George Him, extracts from the 'Schweppshire Post', and profiles of 'Schweppshire Lads who Made Good'. Another Schweppes campaign, featuring a dashing, red-bearded character called Commander Whitehead, was created by David Ogilvy, who also invented 'The Man in the Hathaway Shirt'; a haughty figure with a black eyepatch and a pencil moustache. Both were brand images with conspicuous snob appeal. Even religion became the subject of sophisticated American marketing. 'I am selling the greatest product in the world', declared the Baptist Evangelist Billy Graham, whom two million Britons turned out to hear during his 1953 crusade.

So much was talked about subliminal advertising that people began to doubt their own powers of resistance. In 1958 *Vogue* was writing: 'Having got ourselves thoroughly fussed about subliminal advertising and motivated research – the profitable quarrying of the depth-boys – we might return to ground level and look at the not so deep ideas employed upon our consciousness. The latest thought in cereal packages, expected here from America, is a celluloid gramophone record that can be cut out of the side of the package. Our sample performed, piercingly, "Goofy's Space Trip to the Moon".'

**The Coronation inspired a spate of patriotic 'New Elizabethan era' advertising. *Opposite*, biscuit manufacturers McVitie & Price proudly displayed their royal warrant, and *right*, traditional Daimler skill carried on, 'into a New Elizabethan era, bringing new standards of luxury motoring to many more people in many lands'. 1953.**

Jean Cocteau
My love for Christmas
My Love
Elizabeth Arden
691 FIFTH AVENUE, NEW YORK 22 • PLAZA 3-5846

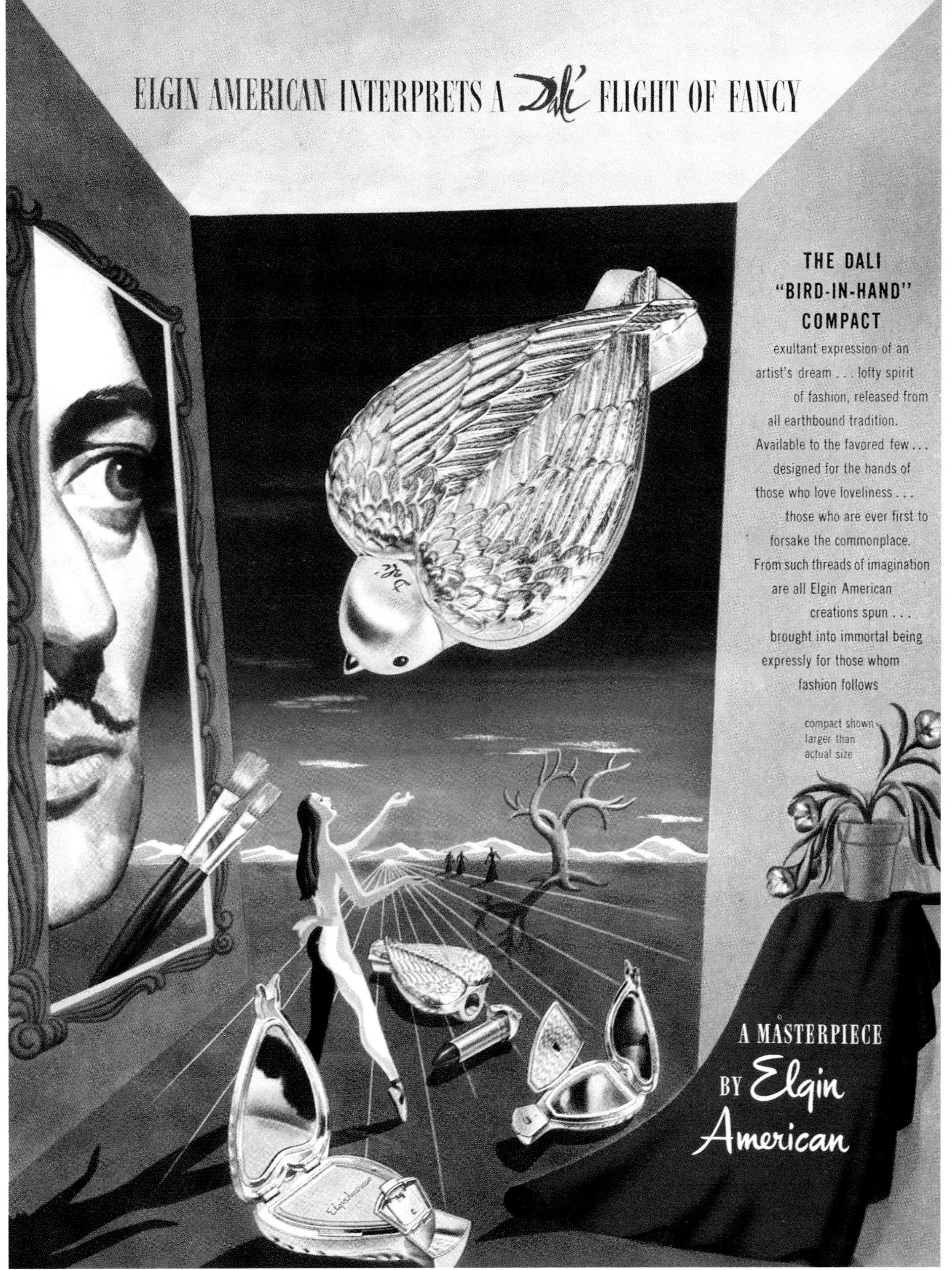


Two fine examples of 'masterpiece' advertising. *Opposite,* in 1950 Jean Cocteau sketched an amorous Adonis for Elizabeth Arden's 'My Love' perfume, and the following year Salvador Dali, *above,* designed a unique 'Bird-in-Hand' compact for Elgin American.

*The Santa Paula sailing through Curacao Harbor . . .*

*Cruise* TO THE CARIBBEAN AND SOUTH AMERICA

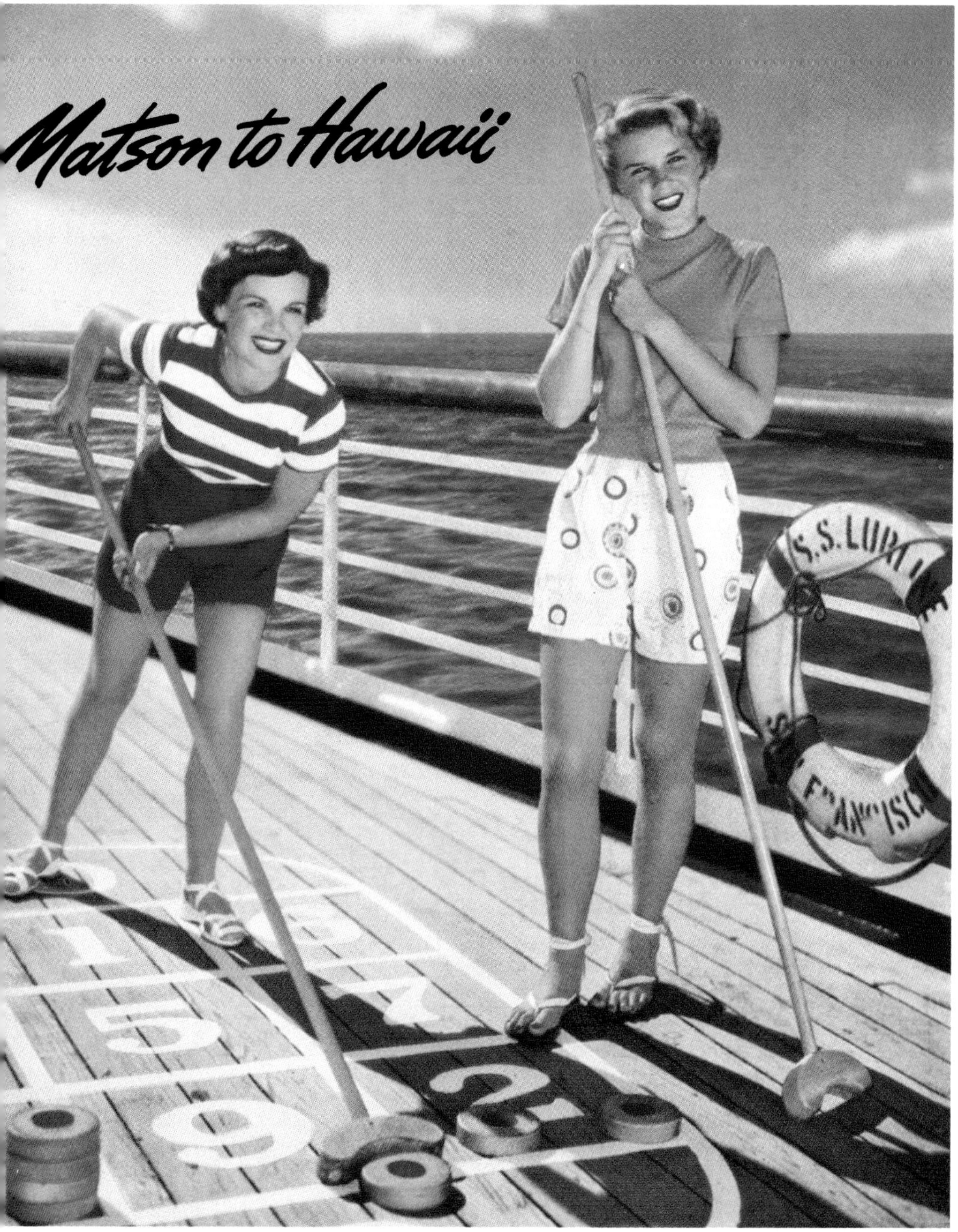

Matson to Hawaii

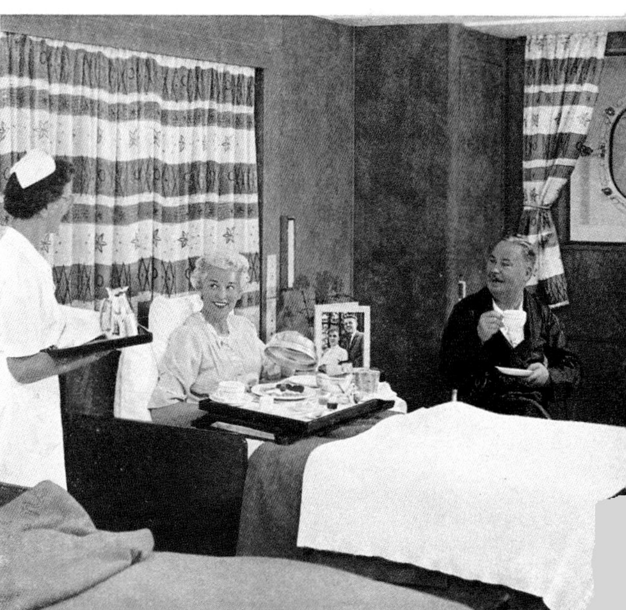

Tomorrow . . . 1500 miles at sea . . .
mother begins her day with a smile

Each day of a Cunard crossing to Europe is an open invitation. The luxury of breakfast in bed . . . games or loafing on the broad decks . . . shopping, dancing and fun . . . time to refresh and plan for a busy schedule after arrival. Whether this is your second honeymoon or your first, what better tonic than the enveloping peace of sea, sky, and ship—the infinite resources of Cunard food and service. Bon voyage—yes, from beginning to end!

*Getting there is half the fun . . . Go* CUNARD

*Widest choice of ships, rates and sailings from New York and Canada to Europe. Consult your travel agent or Cunard Line. Main office in U.S.—25 Broadway, N.Y.*

QUEEN ELIZABETH • QUEEN MARY • MAURETANIA • CARONIA • BRITANNIC • MEDIA • PARTHIA • CARINTHIA • IVERNIA • SAXONIA • SYLVANIA

The advent of jet travel early in the decade marked the end of the luxury liners' heyday; these advertisements were their swansong. *Opposite*, 'Grace Line, serving the Americas with 23 modern 'Santas' and backed by almost a century of experience in building hemisphere trade'. 1950. *Above*, 'For gracious living every moment . . . Cruise to Hawaii on the Lurline'. 1950. *Top right*, 'Everything you've dreamed a holiday should be . . . a joyous round of parties, entertainments, sports . . . enlivened by visits to enchanted tropical isles and the glamorous wonder-cities of South America at the height of their social seasons'. Moore-McCormack. 1952. *Below right*, 'Each day of a Cunard trip to Europe is an open invitation'. 1958.

"88"

All eyes are on the "Rocket"! All eyes are on the most exciting motor car on the highway! It's Oldsmobile's sensational "88"—lowest-priced car with the "Rocket" Engine and Oldsmobile Hydra-Matic*. Try that "Rocket Ride" yourself!

# OLDSMOBILE 88

THE "ROCKET" HYDRA-MATIC CAR!

*Hydra-Matic Drive optional at extra cost on all Oldsmobile models.

A General Motors Value

Car advertisements emphasized value for money, performance, streamlined design and comfort – as well as capitalising on the public's fascination with outer space, *opposite*, 'Oldsmobile's "88", the "Rocket" Hydra-matic car!' 1951. Rootes Motors appealed to British Vogue's style-conscious readers by linking their latest models with those of leading Parisian couturiers: *above*, the Sunbeam Rapier, dress by Jean Dessès. *Below*, the Hillman Minx, dress by Jacques Heim. 1957. *Above right*, 'No matter what you're willing to pay, you'll have a hard time finding any more car than this new Chevrolet wraps into one sweet, low-priced package'. 1959. *Below right*, 'For those who want the very finest in a sports car, Packard presents the Caribbean'. 1953.

*Written by Stephen Potter and drawn by Loudon Sainthill*

**introducing**

# THE FORTY-NINTH STATE

THERE ARE MANY LINKS between Schweppshire and *Schweppsylvania,* 49th State of the U.S. Careful examination of this pictorial map (with historical landmarks) will show that it is much the same as America only more so. The deep South is deeper, with shackier shacks. Its Western *San Franschweppsco* is gayer, and has more artless tramcars. Rich farm lands are quite close to places with No Signs of Life, not to be confused with places where there isn't supposed to be any sign of life, like the *New Schweppsican* desert, which, of course, is living. Even Texas is outdone by *Schweppsas;* and the gentlemanliness of Boston, Mass. is still more so in *Boston, Massachuschweppes,* where the atmosphere is almost reminiscent of what might once have been what once was English.

*SCHWEPPERVESCENCE LASTS THE WHOLE DRINK THROUGH*

*Opposite*, 'Schweppsylvania', an illustration by Loudon Sainthill for Stephen Potter's whimsical Schweppes campaign. 1955. *Above*, 'Refresh ... add zest to the hour ... who ever heard of a better way to offer real refreshment than to serve frosty bottles of delicious Coca-Cola?'. 1950. *Below*, 'Easter's Brightest Idea ... a colourfully original gift – the fashion cigarette. In five glamorous pastel shades ... bleu, saumon, rose, turquoise, bouton d'or'. 1956. *Right*, 'I like du Maurier'. 1958.

# INDEX

**ACKNOWLEDGEMENTS**

My greatest debt for this book is due to *Vogue*'s publisher, Iva Patcévitch, and Edna Woolman Chase, Editor-in-Chief of American, British and French *Vogue*. Together with Condé Nast she made the magazine her life's work, arriving in 1895 as an eighteen-year-old girl and staying for over sixty years, until her death in 1957. Under the art direction of Alexander Liberman the magazine continued to employ the photographers and artists who gave *Vogue* its distinctive character throughout the decade. *Vogue*'s editors of the Fifties were Jessica Daves (America), Audrey Withers (Britain), and Michel de Brunhoff and Edmonde Charles-Roux (France).

I should like to thank Alex Kroll and Carolyn Hall for their invaluable guidance and collaboration at every stage in the creation of *The Fifties in Vogue*. I am also grateful to Victoria Harper and Timothy Hyde for their painstaking research; and to Jane Ross, Robin Muir and Bunny Cantor for their assistance in *Vogue*'s archives. Among others at Condé Nast who contributed in various ways, I would like to mention Sian Dalziel, Meredith Ward and Penny Carmichael, to whom I owe special thanks for typing the manuscript.

I should like to dedicate *The Fifties in Vogue* to my parents.